*The West Coast Trail
and Nitinat Lakes*

The West Coast Trail and Nitinat Lakes

6th Revised Edition

A Trail Guide
by the Sierra Club of Western Canada

Revised and edited by Tim Leadem

DOUGLAS & McINTYRE Vancouver/Toronto

Douglas & McIntyre Ltd.
1615 Venables Street
Vancouver, British Columbia
V5L 2H1

Canadian Cataloguing in Publication Data

Main entry under title:

The West Coast Trail and Nitinat Lakes

ISBN 0-88894-579-5
1. Hiking – British Columbia – West Coast Trail
Guide-books. 2. Hiking – British Columbia Nitinat
Lake Region – Guide-books. 3. West Coast Trail
(B.C.) – Description and travel – Guide-books.
4. Nitinat Lake Region (B.C.) – Description and
travel – Guide-books. I. Sierra Club of
British Columbia.
GV199.44.C22B785   1985   917.11'34   C84-091576-4

Typeset by Ronalds Printing
Printed and bound in Canada by D.W. Friesen & Sons Ltd.

Acknowledgements

THIS BOOK has been a co-operative effort of members of the Sierra Club of British Columbia who love the West Coast Trail and the Nitinat. To Humphrey Davy, Jim Hamilton and Hugh Murray we are indebted for their knowledge of the West Coast Trail and their pioneer efforts to secure park status for it.

The Victoria group of the Sierra Club have been the pioneers of the Nitinat Lakes; they made the early explorations, marked the trails and laboured on the portages. The dedicated efforts of Karen McNaught, Ric Careless, John Willow, Gordy Price, and their supporters, have given us all an inspired example.

This edition was revised and edited by Tim Leadem from the text prepared by John Twigg, Ken Farquharson, Bruce Hardy and Tim Leadem. The editor thanks the employees and wardens of Parks Canada, Pacific Rim National Park, for their helpful comments and information.

Photographs were taken by Steve Cooke, Dean Goodman, John Temple and Bo Martin. Maps for the original edition were drawn by Jerry White and Peter Gose.

Since conditions on the West Coast Trail are continually changing, neither the Sierra Club nor the publisher guarantees the accuracy of the information in this book. You must allow for the unexpected.

*This book is dedicated
to those who, through the years,
have loved this land enough
to fight to preserve
its natural beauty
for future generations.*

NITINAT NARROWS

Contents

TSUSIAT FALLS

— 1 —
Introduction

SINCE THIS BOOK WAS FIRST WRITTEN, in 1972, the West Coast Trail has changed in several ways. At that time, even though usage was increasing dramatically each year, the area was still remote, inviting mostly the "rugged" backpacker. Those rugged backpackers still hike the trail, but more and more they are joined by family groups with children, or by retired people who now have the leisure to enjoy outdoor activity. Responding to the sheer pressure of numbers and to the shift in the types of hikers, Parks Canada has carried out a program of trail repair to eliminate most of the obvious dangers and inconveniences. The hike from Pachena Bay to Carmanah is now a relatively safe and easy one; from Carmanah to Port Renfrew is relatively safe though not necessarily easy. There are still dangers for the unwary hiker. Whereas the trail is still a challenge to the average hiker, it is no longer the true wilderness it once was. For some this change is distressing because it removes a challenge which cannot be replaced; for others it means the opportunity to experience an area they may have been reluctant to enter a few years ago. One negative aspect of change, though, is the increase in litter and vandalism caused by the carelessness or ignorance of hikers uneducated in trail courtesy. This problem can only get worse unless every hiker develops a personal sense of stewardship for the trail.

This new edition has been written with two main purposes in mind: to help hikers of all ranges of experience and ability enjoy the West Coast Trail, and to convey to everyone a sense of urgency for protecting the quality of experience which it offers. Towards those purposes, here is advice about potential dangers to you and to the trail.

PERSONAL CAUTIONS

1. Tell someone where you are going and your expected day of arrival at your destination. There are still places where you could get lost or injured without anyone's knowledge. Be sure to register in and upon your return at the information centres.

2. Be equipped. Once on the trail, you are about 70 km (45 miles) from its end and fresh supplies. Suggested equipment is listed in Chapter Five.

3. Be equipped for rain. Even on the sunniest of days, the hiker may encounter bad weather on the west coast of Vancouver Island. Within hours a front can move in bringing cold air, strong winds and torrential rains. Rain gear will be your most important item of equipment, and should be adequate to keep your person and your sleeping bag dry. You should know the meaning and symptoms of hypothermia — a condition which can sneak up on you and which is the greatest single cause of death among amateur hikers. It is discussed in Chapter Eight.

4. Respect the sea. It is unbelievably powerful and can catch you unawares. The worst danger is from the occasional freak Pacific swell tumbling up surge channels or rising dramatically over rocks. People have been literally plucked off rocks they were exploring by these sudden swells. A special danger spot is Nitinat Narrows, where you can be temporarily marooned if there is no one to boat you across. Very fast incoming or, especially, outgoing currents mix with the ocean breakers, and many people have drowned there in the last century. In fact, all of Nitinat Lake is noted for dangerous winds. Finally, be wary of tides. More than one camper has set up a tent well away from the water, especially near a river mouth, only to find himself and his gear afloat in the middle of the night. A more serious situation is hiking the shore at low tide, finding your progress barred by a cliff and your return prevented by an incoming tide. See Chapter Eight for a discussion of tide tables.

5. Carry a water bottle. There are parts of the trail where, in the dry season, you might walk for several hours without finding good water. Although this is unusual, it is better to be overcautious than sorry.

6. Respect rocks, cliffs and slippery logs. There are still some hazards even on "improved" parts, and there will always be hazards off the main trail. Slips on logs or rocks can result in serious injuries. On some parts of the main trail, one step to the side is a hundred-foot drop. The lack of good traction soles on your hiking boots will multiply the dangers. So will too heavy a pack.

Rotten boardwalks are now a rarity on the main trail, but you may encounter them on side trails. A good technique for crossing all rotten boardwalks is to step on two boards at once, or step above the log supports. If the walk is tilted, you should walk on the side nearest the ground, unless the boards are slippery, in which case it might be best to hike off the boards. Maintaining a medium speed allows you to keep going forward instead of down if a board should break.

7. Comfortable, sturdy hiking boots are essential. Next to rain gear, they are the most critical items for safe hiking.

8. Carry waterproof matches, or some other form of fire starting device.

9. Carry a first aid kit.

If 4,000 people pass through an area in a season and each does a little damage, the result is a lot of damage. On the other hand, if each does no damage, the sum will be no damage. It is easy to visit an area, use it and enjoy it, yet leave behind no sign of your visit.

1. Pack out your garbage. The rule for all wilderness areas is: "If you can carry it in, you can carry it out." "It" includes polyethylene sheets, tin cans, bottles, plastic, and those modern sources of "aluminum pollution," freeze-dried food packages. Just burying garbage is not satisfactory, given the number of people who use the trail. Burnable garbage should be thoroughly burned, both for aesthetic reasons and to avoid attracting animals. Human solid wastes should be buried.

2. Each party should carry its own shelter. The few cabins still standing along the trail are in poor condition. A lean-to made in the forest destroys a small part of that forest, and several lean-tos destroy a larger part. Whereas beach lean-tos are less destructive because they can be made from driftwood, you are not really helping people have their own "wilderness experience" if you leave a shelter for them. Most people who hike the trail want to test their own self-reliance.

Unless you have no choice, do not hack new campsites out of the bush; use ones that are already developed. A general rule for beach camping is to camp below the winter high tide line and, of course, above the summer high tide line.

3. Take from the land only what you need. The West Coast Trail is a microcosm of modern civilization. When there were only a few people, the area provided abundant resources and could withstand almost any damage. That is no longer true. The time may come when restrictions are put on plant and animal use, or use of the trail itself. The best way to avoid that is to be moderate: use only what you need; don't waste.

4. Respect private holdings. Apart from a few inholdings, the main private lands in the park are Indian lands, including the villages at Port Renfrew, Clo-oose, Whyac, and Pachena Bay. The vandalism in these areas has been increasing yearly. Houses, which may or may not be in seasonal use, have been damaged. The Indians at Whyac have lost at least two boats, "borrowed" by hikers, then carelessly allowed to drift out to sea. The Indians also use areas outside of the communities, for fishing or other activities; these areas are clearly marked on the maps in this book. As original inhabitants of the province, the Indians are part of the history of the West Coast Trail, and their holdings should be respected.

5. Remember that large groups have more environmental impact on the trail than small groups and more social impact on other campers. Parks Canada recommends a maximum group size of eight.

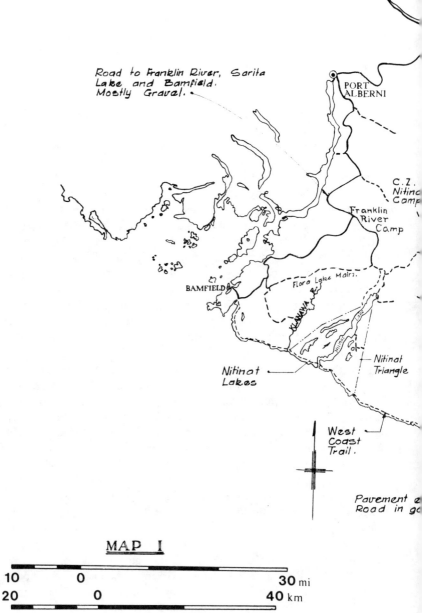

Road to Franklin River, Sarita
Lake and Bamfield.
Mostly Gravel.

PORT
ALBERNI

C.Z.
Nitina
Camp

Franklin
River
Camp

Flora Lake Mahr.

BAMFIELD

KLANAWA

NITINAT

Nitinat
Lakes

Nitinat
Triangle

West
Coast
Trail.

Pavement a
Road in go

MAP I

| 10 | 0 | 30 mi |
| 20 | 0 | 40 km |

12

See following companies for maps of logging roads:

Port Alberni - Nitinat: MacMillan Bloedel
Lake Cowichan - Nitinat: B.C. Forest Products
Port Renfrew: B.C. Forest Products

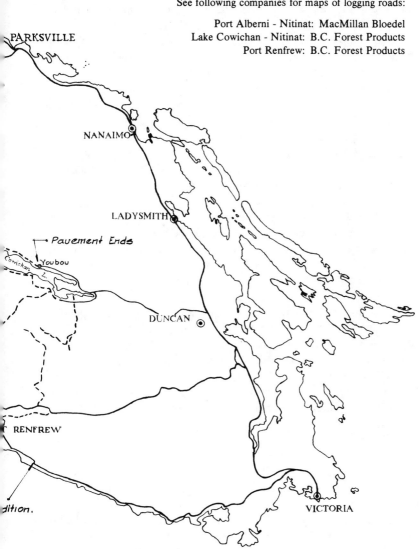

PARKSVILLE

NANAIMO

LADYSMITH

Pavement Ends

Cowichan   Youbou
L.

DUNCAN

RENFREW

dition.

VICTORIA

13

In 1971 more than 2,000 people hiked the entire trail between Port Renfrew and Bamfield, and many more spent a day or two exploring portions of it. In the summer of 1986, over 10,000 signed the registers at the Parks Canada Information Centres at Pachena Bay and Port Renfrew, and many others either didn't sign or hiked other sections. This count, though it may seem irrelevant, is important in the continuing controversy regarding the trail's eventual protected status.

The West Coast Trail became a political football in the summer of 1970 when it was included in Pacific Rim National Park. But the trail and the rugged coastline have been in the news since the mid-1800s. About 60 ships of all sizes have foundered along this portion of British Columbia's coast since 1854, including the *M. V. Vanlene,* which ran aground in 1974, spilling oil on the beaches of Cape Beale, just north of Pachena. The submerged wreck still occasionally seeps oil, and points up the concern about the vulnerability of the coastline to oil spills.

In fact, so many ships drifted with the currents around Cape Flattery and slammed into the cruel rock shelves that the area became known as the "Graveyard of the Pacific." As well, the area has been a graveyard for many people. Indians have lived and fought and died on the coast since well before the first white men sailed past the island. And many people have lost their lives in shipwrecks. In 1906, the wreck of the S. S. *Valencia,* just north of the Klanawa River, took the lives of 126 people. It was this wreck that spurred the federal government of the time to improve what was then little more than an animal path and make it a lifesaving trail. It was maintained for years by solitary linemen: rugged, independent men who worked alone, keeping the trail open in order to fix the telephone line on the frequent occasions when it was knocked out by windfalls. Until the 1950s, they and the lighthouse keepers were the only permanent white residents outside of the villages.

The trail has been in the news for other reasons besides shipwrecks. As long ago as 1926, when the land resource in British Columbia seemed infinite, the recreation potential of the Nitinat and coast area was recognized, and a park reserve established. The reserve was lifted in 1947 because the government of the time considered the region too remote to be usable for recreation. A struggle then broke out within the forest industry for its control. First it was set up as the Clayoquot Cutting Circle, where small independent operators could work. However, the major companies had designs on the area, and in 1967 the Clayoquot Circle was disbanded and the area put into Tree Farm Licences 21 and 27, managed by MacMillan Bloedel and British Columbia Forest Products.

But the Nitinat and the west coast were still remote, and the timber on the land very old, much of it past its prime, so the forest companies did not begin to penetrate the area until after 1965, when they had exhausted more profitable forest lands. By this time hikers had become aware of the beauty of the area and were using the old trail despite it poor state. They were helped by the Provincial Parks Branch, which cleared and marked some of the worst sections at the south end. At the same time, a number of people, notably Bruce Scott of Bamfield and Jim Hamilton of Clo-oose, were publicizing the trail and urging its protection.

Because the trail was being used by growing numbers, the federal government was pressing the provincial government to include it and a few adjacent river basins in the Pacific Rim National Park. These efforts bore fruit. The park was created in April 1970 and included three portions: Long Beach, Broken Group Islands, and the West Coast Trail. The boundaries of the trail portion were left to be decided at a later date.

From 1970 to 1972, vigorous controversy took place over two issues. One was the desire of many people, including the Sierra Club, to have the so-called Nitinat Triangle (the Hobiton-Tsusiat-Squalicum watershed) preserved from logging, and the equally strong determination of the provincial government of the day and the logging companies to log the area. The other was a campaign to have the boundaries of the trail widened, in order at least to protect the trail from the sight and sound of logging, and from blowdowns. The campaign, led by the Sierra Club, was long, hard and sometimes bitter, and when the first edition of this book was written, the conclusion was still in doubt. This doubt was thought to have been removed in August of 1972, when the provincial government announced that it would preserve the Nitinat Lakes from logging and would widen the proposed trail boundaries. That commitment was a compromise between desirability and economics, and was still inadequate to protect the trail fully from logging, four-wheel drive vehicles, etc.

In fact, doubt still exists. It would seem that wild, empty Vancouver Island, and much of B. C. for that matter, is so committed to logging that there is little other comparable land with which to compensate the companies for the loss of their cutting rights in this area — in spite of the fact that 95 per cent of B. C.'s land is owned by the public! And the situation is worse in other desirable wilderness areas such as the Tsitika, the Stein, and South Moresby Islands.

Negotiations between logging companies and provincial government and the province and federal government appear to be concluded. The boundaries are apparently established, but they might not be wide enough to completely protect the wilderness nature of the trail. At some places, logging roads may come to within 400 metres or less of the trail. Protection of main access points such as the Klanawa, Cheewhat and Carmanah rivers may still be uncertain. Parks Canada is presently administering the trail as best it can without full legal authority. It is anticipated that the trail will officially become part of Pacific Rim National Park some time in 1987/88. More detail on the history and conservation efforts directed to the trail are given in Chapter Nine.

This book describes the hike from Port Renfrew to Bamfield, guiding the hiker over the hardest section first. Occasionally, notes are inserted which will be of special interest to hikers going the other way. Also, the Nitinat Lakes, though geographically connected with the trail, are usually done as a separate canoeing trip, and so are described in a separate section.

In this introduction we have tried to outline the main themes which this book will develop. First, it is a guidebook to help you enjoy the trail — to respect its dangers and appreciate its beauties. Second, we hope to give you an appreciation of the tremendous work and dedication which have gone to make the trail what it is today. Third, we hope to convince everybody of how easily the values of the trail can be spoiled. Some say it is already being ruined; only present and future hikers will decide the truth of this judgement.

Parks Canada has basically finished upgrading the main trail, although the southern third, from Carmanah to Port Renfrew, still has some rough spots. The West Coast is a dynamic biological zone, and the forest grows very quickly, so there is no such thing as a permanent, finished trail. Read carefully the hints given in the trail guide and in subsequent chapters, but don't stake your life on them, since conditions can change from year to year. The most important thing to carry with you, even more important than good equipment, is a large dose of common sense.

The main organization and information of the first edition has not been altered. One change has been made, though: hiking times have been eliminated. Hikers vary so considerably in their abilities and ambitions that our previous estimates were not very helpful. When you have been on the trail for a few hours, you will be able to gauge your hiking speed. Towards evening, double your estimate to allow time before darkness. The trail can be hiked in a few days if you really want to rush, but you will miss so much scenery that it is hardly worth it.

From all those who have contributed to this guide, good luck with the weather and enjoy your hike.

— 2 —
The West Coast Trail

TO REACH THE TRAILHEAD at Port Renfrew you must either drive, in which case you will have to return there to retrieve your car, or hitchhike. There is no public transportation. Routes, accommodation and sources of information are discussed in Chapter Four.

The upgrading of the West Coast Trail has been basically completed. However, you should not approach the trail complacently, especially if you are a beginner. Even though the challenges that used to thrill — or terrorize — hikers have mainly been removed, you can still encounter the following: mud, slippery logs, slippery rocks, washouts, high rivers, high tides, sudden ocean surges, dropoffs, steep banks, windfalls, overgrown sections, darkness on the trail, high winds and torrential rains. It is even possible to lose the trail if, for example, a windfall forces you to detour away from a winding section. If you are not comfortable about these kinds of inconveniences, you probably should not attempt to make this hike. If, on the other hand, you are willing to rough it a little and adapt to nature's whims, by all means prepare well and go ahead. You may be delighted at how easy it is, after all.

All things being equal, you will probably prefer hiking the beach where possible. But beach walking on loose sand or gravel can be exhausting, and walking on wet, algae-covered boulders can be precarious, so use your judgement. Above all, take note of the places listed in this guide where you could be caught by an incoming tide.

To enter the trail at the southern end you need a boat; the Gordon River is too deep and wide to wade. On the eastern side of the river, the land belongs to the Pacheenaht Indian Band, and usually the Indians will ferry you across. For specific information, see Chapter Four.

If you use your own boat, be forewarned that Port San Juan is not as sheltered and gentle as it sometimes looks. Near the shore, from the San Juan River to the mouth of the Gordon River, the water can build up into surprisingly steep breakers. When approaching by boat, stay well away from shore and study the pattern of the swells. Also, take note that it is not always easy to get ashore at Thrasher Cove.

From Gordon River to Thrasher Cove the trail stays in the woods, well away from the beach, which is impassable because of cliffs. Any difficulties you encounter on the south portion of the trail will mainly depend upon the weather before or during your hike. If it has been rainy, you should expect mud of varying depths, and log crossings over numerous small streams will be slippery. The hiking is mostly on the flat or is a gentle up and down. When you pass the old donkey engine, a relic of former logging, you will be about halfway to Thrasher Cove. Note that the forest around the southern portion of the trail is second growth, which accounts for the dense underbrush not found in other parts of the trail. From here to Thrasher Cove the climbs are steeper, both up and down. At several points there are openings in the forest which give excellent views of Port San Juan and the distant Olympic Mountains in Washington. The openings give relief from the steady hike through forest.

A good campsite is found about 15 feet off the main trail at its highest point; follow a huge log and an old logging cable. There is room for at least four tents. This campsite has a fine view of the ocean and the distant Olympics; an especially beautiful sight is to watch the rising sun dissipate the heavy mists at the lower levels of the mountain. However, the nearest water is at [8], which may be dry in arid summers, and is reached by a steep and difficult path. So if you plan to camp at this site, fill your water bottles at one of the streams after passing the donkey engine.

After the high point at [7] the trail drops steeply to a small creek. There is an old log crossing here which was used for many years. If it has not been improved, you might prefer to descend to the creek and pick your way across. If the creek is running high, you may have to use the old crossing anyhow, in which case a rope handline is a good psychological crutch. A suspension bridge is planned.

After the campsite, the trail is steep and scenically undistinguished except for the beauty of the forest floor. At [10] a series of log ladders leads to or from Thrasher Cove. You should face inward when using all ladders encountered on the trail and make sure of your footing on the sometimes muddy rungs. There is good camping at this cove. The west Thrasher Cove trail [13] has been abandoned and is very rough.

The trail from Thrasher Cove to 150 Yard Creek can be slow going. At low tide you can hike along the shore. It is slow and tedious travel amongst slippery, algae-covered boulders at first, but once the shelf is reached at [14] it is fast and easy. Remember, though, that this alternative is only possible at low tide.

The campsite at 150 Yard Creek is small and extremely wet, but it is a useful place to camp if you don't have time to make it to Camper Bay.

A side trail a few minutes out of the 150 Yard campsite leads to a

A side trail a few minutes out of the 150 Yard campsite leads to a rocky shelf on the coast. At low tide it is possible to walk along the shelf, but be sure that the tide will stay out long enough to allow you to reach the next access to the main trail at [20, 23]. One problem with walking along the shelf is that in several areas it is broken by sea chasms or surge channels. It is usually possible to outflank these by using rough bypass trails. However, it is impossible to hike all the way to Camper Bay, so you should regain the main trail at [23]. The trail between [18] and [26] is often boggy, since all the mountain runoff collects here. This is the time that you will be looking forward to the dry socks in your pack.

The once-legendary blowdown area is now much improved. It still consists of trees blown on top of each other, but except under extremely wet conditions, you probably won't have any particular problem in getting through.

Such blowdown areas will become more common if the government permits logging companies to operate less than half a mile from the shoreline. The trees protect each other from such blowdowns by wind pruning: growing evenly so that the strong ocean winds pass overhead instead of swirling into open spaces. A good example of this pruning can be seen from the tidal marker at the beginning of the trail. A wedge of salal growing from the first trees right down to the beach has created a protective belt.

Another series of ladders leads down to Camper Creek. There is now a cable car for getting across the creek during high water. If the creek is low you can wade across, but if you have any doubts on either your ability or the possible danger of the high water, then you should use the cable car, for this river is dangerous. Generally, wading across is quicker and easier, given the right conditions.

There are a number of techniques for stream crossing. One is to remove your boots and pants and wade across, using a staff for balance. (Use driftwood or other dead wood. Remember, live trees have feelings.) Because the water is cold and the rocks slippery, many hikers put their boots back on (without socks). Others carry a pair of light sneakers expressly for crossing streams. And there are always a few who say, "What the heck!" and wade in fully clothed. There are also the ones who spend all evening shivering around a fire while they try to dry out their clothes. Remember that wet socks sometimes cause blisters.

Camper Bay is a good campsite. However, like others, it tends to become overcrowded during peak season (June to August). This, of course, brings a problem with trail aesthetics. It bears repeating that you are in a wilderness area and are directly responsible for the disposal of the waste you create.

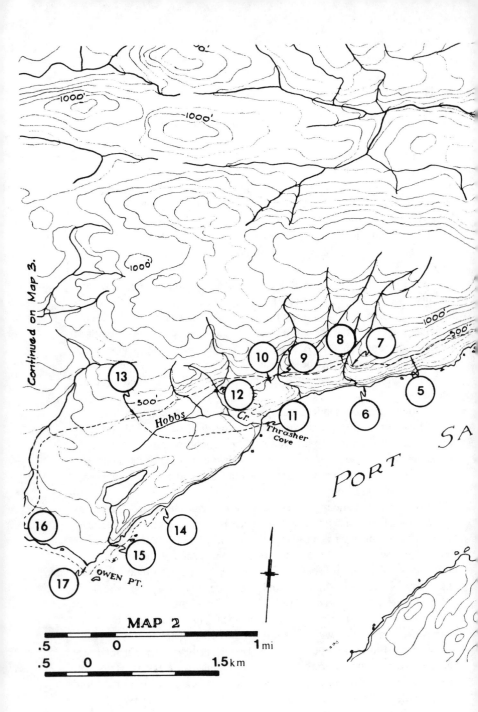

Continued on Map 3.

Hobbs Cr.

Thrasher Cove

OWEN PT.

PORT SA

MAP 2

.5   0   1 mi
.5   0   1.5 km

20

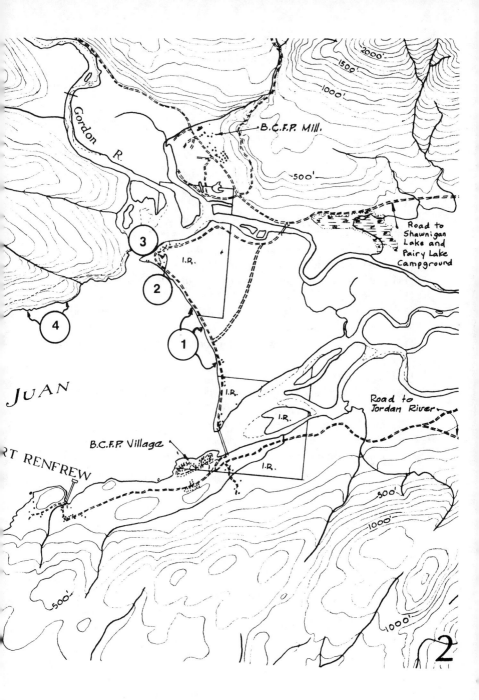

Gordon R.

B.C.F.P. Mill.

2000'
1500'
1000'
500'

Road to
Shawnigan
Lake and
Fairy Lake
Campground

③

②

④

①

I.R.

I.R.

JUAN

I.R.

Road to
Jordan River

I.R.

B.C.F.P. Village

I.R.

RT RENFREW

500'

1000'

500'

1000'

2

21

[1] *Wide sandy beach. Good camping.*

[2] *Pacheenaht Indian Reserve, where you can get a boat across the Gordon River or to Thraser Cove.*

[3] *Bulletin Board, beginning of West Coast Trail.*

[4] *Dense vegetation on forest floor because of second growth forest. It is easy to lose the trail in this area.*

[5] *Old donkey engine left from former logging.*

[6] *Steep gravel slope just below trail. Beach access in emergency. Beware of landslides.*

[7] *Highest point on trail, small campsite, water usually at [8]. Between [6] and [7] trail passes through open areas with good views.*

[8] *Small creek crossed on log. Trail steep on both sides of creek.*

[9] *Log Jam Creek. Pleasant rest stop, possible campsite.*

[10] *Intersection of east trail to Thrasher Cove. Steep.*

[11] *Thrasher Cove. Excellent camping. Water at Hobbs Creek.*

[12] *Pretty falls, but difficult access.*

[13] *Former west access trail to Thrasher Cove, now abandoned. Use east ladders at #10.*

[14] *Sandstone shelf begins. Beach hiking at low tide only. Relatively fast to west of here, slow to east.*

[15] *Cleft falls.*

[16] *150 Yard Creek. Good, small campsite. Interesting with pool and cavern below campsite.*

[17] *Owen Point. Possible to walk around point if tide below 6 feet (1.8 m). A trail exists over point. Area to west known as ''Moonscape'' because of unusual eroded sandstone.*

Between Camper Bay and Sandstone Creek you have a choice of hiking either along the beach or on the trail. The beach route is easier to hike but is only passable when the tide is very low — below 4 ft. (1.2 m). At medium tides the shelf will be covered, and even at low tide you may have to do some wading in getting off the shelf at Sandstone Creek. There is a fixed wire cable on your right to help you scramble up the slippery waterfall just before you meet the trail.

From Camper Bay make sure that you have enough low tide time to at least regain the trail along the creek bed [33]. If you are inexperienced or doubtful about the tide it is probably best to stay on the trail.

If you do elect to hike the trail from Camper Bay you must first climb the ladders behind the campsite. From there it is fairly routine slogging to [33] where you have a choice of rejoining the beach or staying on the trail.

The trail from [33] to Cullite Creek is easy and can usually be done quickly. Cullite Cove offers a beautiful campsite on the southeast side of the creek, but the creek gulley is usually so wet that it is difficult to maintain a cooking fire. In such cases, a small gas stove is worth its weight in your pack.

The trail from Cullite to Logan goes through a large bog. You should stay on the boardwalk, not only to save yourself from taking a mud bath but also to protect the fragile environment around you. Most of the plants in this area are fighting for their survival in the high acid and low nitrogen environment. Hopefully the damage from thousands of former hikers slogging through deep mud will gradually repair itself.

Once across the bog you face a steep descent by ladders to Logan Creek, which is spanned by an attractive suspension bridge. If you are travelling in a large group, note the precaution that only six people at a time should be on the bridge. The present Logan Creek suspension bridge is a replacement for the previous one which was destroyed by high winds in 1981.

There is good camping on the Bamfield side of the Logan Creek beach. Under an average flow, the creek is not difficult to cross. It is easiest near the mouth, and by using the logs you can avoid soaking your boots. Logan Creek is a good place to stop for lunch, wait for a low tide, or spend the night. There is good beachcombing here, being the most southerly beach along the trail that collects flotsam from the open ocean. Keep and eye out for glass fishing floats which drift across from the Orient.

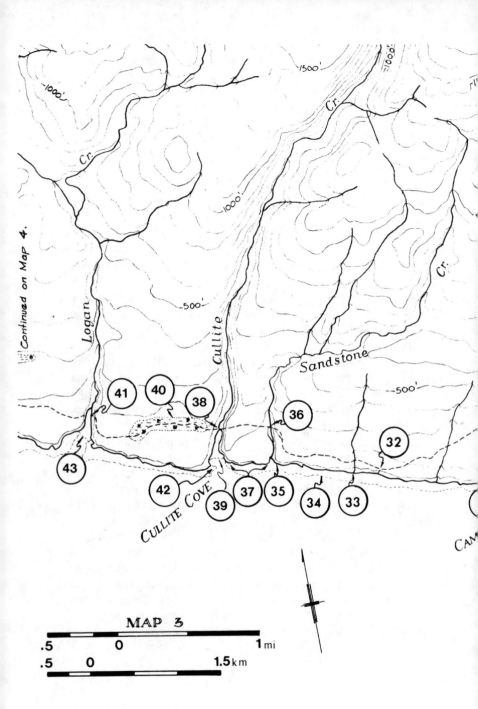

Continued on Map 4.

1500'

1000'

Cr.

Cr.

Cr.

Logan

Cullite

1000'

500'

Sandstone

500'

41

40

38

36

32

43

42

39

37

35

34

33

CULLITE COVE

CAM

MAP 3

.5   0   1 mi

.5   0   1.5 km

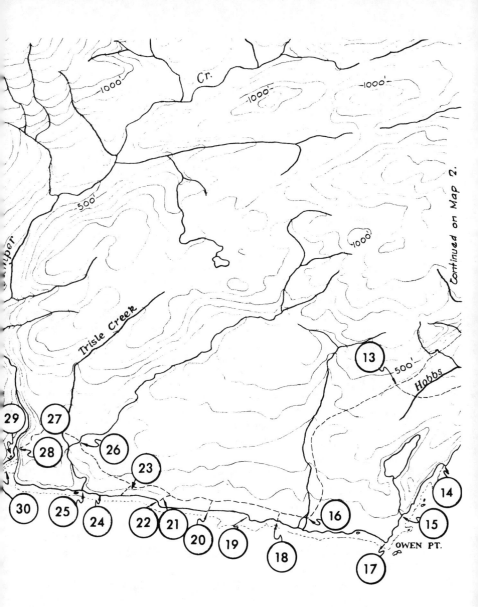

Cr.

1000'

1000'

1000'

500'

1000'

Juniper

Continued on Map 2.

Trisle Creek

13

500'

Hobbs

29

27

28

26

23

30

25

24

22

21

20

19

18

16

14

15

OWEN PT.

17

3

25

[18] *Beach access trail.*

[19] *Small shady cove.*

[20] *Beach access. Shelf from [20] to [23] is impassable at high tide.*

[21] *Small trail to edge of cliff.*

[22] *Small shady cove.*

[23] *Last beach access trail before Trisle Creek. Use caution.*

[24] *Tidal pool area, rich marine life. Good swimming at right tide.*

[25] *Sandstone shelf ends in deep, wide, impassable channel. Possible to climb around behind with difficulty, but two chasms side by side prevent beach access to Camper Bay. Good camping at mouth of Trisle Creek.*

[26] *Small campsite on creek. Waterfall short way upstream. Slippery log.*

[27] *"Blowdown" area. Follow easy route over logs.*

[28] *Camper Creek. Cable car crossing. River dangerous in high water.*

[29] *Resumption of trail.*

[30] *Camper Bay has excellent camping areas and a cable car. Beach accesses to and from Camper Bay are potentially hazardous, especially at high tides.*

[31] *Sandstone shelf broken by channel which is impassable at high tide. If this is passable, the rest of the route to Sandstone Creek will also be passable (provided that you do not have a rapid incoming tide). A bypass trail has been cut over the break.*

[32] *Short trail to cliff's edge. Beautiful view.*

[33] *Beach access from trail down this creek bed.*

[34] *Seals often sighted here.*

[35] *Sandstone shelf ends. Access to trail up creek bed. Climb off shelf onto rocks and into ocean (will be thigh-deep at most if [31] is passable). It is very hard to climb up onto this shelf, and therefore hikers going towards Port Renfrew should take the trail. To get back to the trail, cross over creek on log jam and continue walking up to 15-foot waterfall. Trail crosses creek immediately upstream from waterfall.*

[36] *Sandstone Creek crossing. Good rest stop but no campsite.*

[37] *This portion of sandstone shelf cannot be reached while carrying pack.*

[38] *Cullite Creek. Cable car crossing.*

[39] *Cullite Cove. Beautiful campsite, unreachable when creek is high.*

[40] *"The bog." Little forest cover. Stay on boardwalk. Botanically interesting.*

[41] *Logan Creek. Suspension bridge. River dangerous when high.*

[42] *Shelf cut by deep wide channel. Impassable. The rest of the shelf is not very interesting.*

Between Logan and Walbran creeks, you have a choice of the trail route (slow and uninteresting but not difficult) and the potentially dangerous beach route which should be used only when tides are below 6 feet and seas are calm. The tide problem is at [44] where a deep sea chasm runs all the way to the cliff. The chasm can be crossed only if the waves are small and the tide is low enough to expose a rock in the middle. Even if the rock is exposed, it is usually slippery, so that it is best to slither around the edge of the chasm, preferably with the assistance of ropes. The crossing is further complicated by a waterfall which makes all the rocks slippery. It should not be attempted by inexperienced hikers. A few other sea chasms in this area may present some problems.

Walbran Creek is usually crossed via the cable car. There is an excellent "swimming hole" just upstream of the cable crossing, but because soap is contributing to an algae problem in the creek, we urge you to use a biodegradable kind.

At the Walbran there is plenty of open space for tents, and an adequate supply of firewood, but the wind coming off the ocean at night is usually cold and moist.

From the Walbran it is only a few hundred yards to a long, sandy beach. Hiking from here to Carmanah along the beach looks easy, but the sand is so fine that you must learn a new style of walking. After a while you will discover where the sand is hardest. Try the water's edge or at high tide marks and in darker sand. When the tide is out, the rock shelf also provides good hiking. A bypass trail has been built around Vancouver Point, which could be an obstacle at high tide.

If you get tired of hiking the beach there is a good trail from the Walbran to Vancouver Point, about a mile and a quarter (2 km), and from Kulaht Creek to Bonilla Creek. A bridge spans Bonilla Creek and a cable car crosses the Carmanah River, but at low water you will not necessarily need to use them. There is good camping around the Carmanah River, but many other parts of that wide sweeping beach are clogged with driftwood.

After crossing Carmanah River, proceed on the beach until it ends. Here you will see a trail opening between alder trees which leads to a ladder. The trail climbs over the headland behind Carmanah and through the forest to the next beach. It is best not to enter the lighthouse compound unless you wish to take photographs or to go back to the water. The water route involves a lot of scrambling over large and slippery rocks and is passable only at low tides.

The section from Carmanah to Klanawa is, in the opinion of many hikers, the most scenic part of the trail. Not only does the terrain alternate between forest and coastline but also the cliffs are less continuous, offering more opportunity for beach exploration. We have listed only some of the beach access points.

BEACH NEAR NITINAT NARROWS

At the Bay of the Cribs, the hiking is easy by either beach or forest. At the south end of the bay there is a prominent headland which is visible almost to Nitinat Narrows. It is possible to continue along the shelves here to Dare Point and beyond, but only at low tide, and there are few points where you can regain the trail. At [55] a surge channel and ledge block the way, but a rough detour has been slashed through the salal. There are ladders from the trail to the beach about 100 yards (90 m) north of the surge channel. The trail from the Cribs rises steeply and goes along the top of the cliff almost to Dare Point, then comes back to near sea level. The telegraph wires close to the trail here are phone links from Whyac and Clo-oose. Please do not damage them. After descending the long flight of stairs above the beach, hikers may regain the beach at the end of the boardwalk. A campsite with water is located at the south end of the sandy beach.

From here to the Cheewhat the trail goes over old sand dunes which have been colonized by forest. There are lots of flat, sheltered campsites along the trail and also camping spots on the beach. Water is a bit of a problem; the nearest places to fill your bottles are the north side of the Cheewhat Bridge or at the south end of this long beach.

If you elect to walk along the beach, you may miss the point where the trail turns to the right through the forest to the Cheewhat Bridge. If you wish to camp near the mouth of the Cheewhat, you should continue along the beach. Although this is Indian Reserve, so far camping has been permitted here. In the past, people who were staying a length of time constructed large, unsightly shelters of driftwood and plastic. These intrude upon the scenery, and you should feel free to dismantle them if they block a campsite you would like to use. (The plastic can be burned.) As you approach the Cheewhat, you will see many signs of former settlement. There are also private dwellings in this area.

The Cheewhat is a slow-flowing tidal river called "river of urine" by the Indians because of its colour and bad taste. Better drinking water is available from the many small creeks in the Clo-oose and Cheewhat area, notably a small creek at the north end of the bridge. This creek may be dry in arid summers. The suspension bridge across the Cheewhat was new in 1976 and is a favorite subject of photographers. Cheewhat Lake is a wintering ground for rare trumpeter swams. (A word of warning: If you should approach the Cheewhat River by boat, be careful. Under certain tide and wind conditions, especially at low tide, it can have dangerous standing waves. These occur when the speed of outflow nearly matches the speed of the incoming breakers, and the waves become very slow and steep. This warning applies to almost any exposed shore or river entrance along the west coast, but the dangers are often less evident at the bars of calm rivers.)

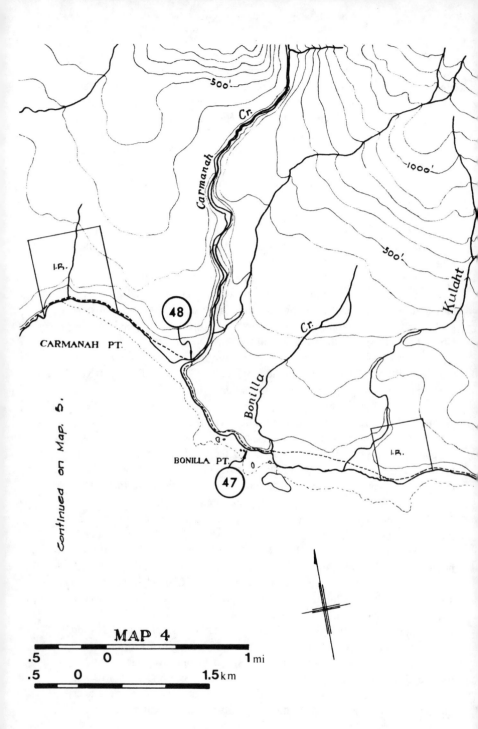

500'

Carmanah Cr.

1000'

500'

Kulaht

I.B.

48

Cr.

CARMANAH PT.

Bonilla

Continued on Map. 5.

BONILLA PT.

I.B.

47

MAP 4

| .5 | 0 | 1 mi |

| .5 | 0 | 1.5 km |

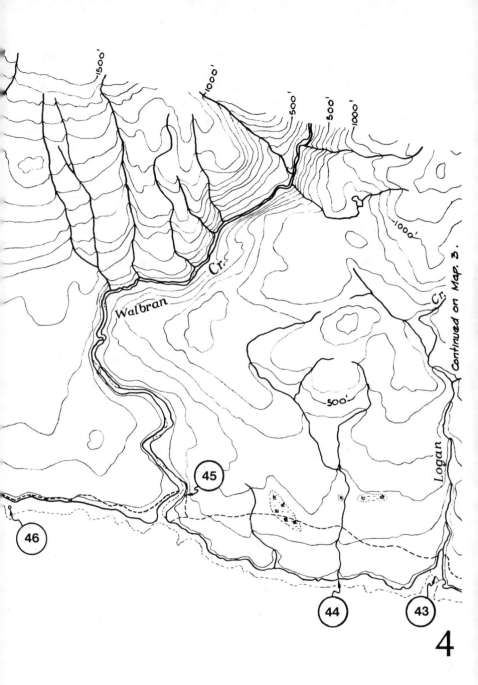

1500'
1000'
500'
500'
1000'
-1000'
Cr.
Walbran
Cr.
Continued on Map. 3.
Logan
500'
45
46
44
43

4

[43] *Good campsite on beach by creek, unreachable when creek is high. It is possible to walk from here to Clo-oose at low tide. If going in opposite direction, note [44].*

[44] *Waterfall and channel in sandstone shelf: very slippery. Passable only at low tide (below 5.5 feet), in dry weather and with calm seas.*

[45] *Walbran Creek. Excellent campsite, good swimming. Creek is impassable and dangerous when high. Crossed by cable car. Beach walk from here to Carmanah Lighthouse is passable at high tide, best at low tide.*

[46] *Vancouver Point. It may be necessary to take bypass route around this at high tide.*

[47] *Bonilla Point is marked by a huge triangular sign sticking out of the bush. This sign is a navigational aid which corresponds to one at Cape Flattery on the Olympic Peninsula.*

[48] *Carmanah Creek. Good camping on lighthouse side of creek.*

This area has many signs of former and present settlement. Clo-oose itself has always been an Indian village. In the 1880s, William Grove obtained an acre of land where the "A" frame now is, before the boundaries of the Indian Reservation were established in 1892. In the 1890s, William Stone came as the first missionary; the Logan family were early settlers. In 1912 a land development began, and several dozen white people settled, mainly to the east and west of Clo-oose. The white hut now occupied by a caretaker is the former United Church chapel.

Clo-oose residents, along with the lighthouse keepers and the linemen, often played heroic roles in the rescue of shipwrecked mariners. This small community, as did so many others, contributed a disproportionate share of young men in World War I, and after that the community declined. Other factors were isolation, the closing of the cannery on Nitinat Lake, the decline of the salmon fishery, and in the 1950s the withdrawal of the coastal steamer *Maquinna* as many west coast communities became accessible by road or float plane. The last of the original white families left in 1952.

Scattered around this area are various mementoes of the past, including houses, gardens and gravestones. Many of the houses were abandoned "as is," for it was too difficult to move out the furnishings. Weather and vandals have left them in a deplorable state. Nevertheless, they represent a museum of the history of the trail and should not be damaged further.

If you have trouble finding water near Clo-oose, a good source is located along the Brown Bay trail a few hundred feet from [59] down the hill. It is marked by a sign. There is also plenty of good camping in this area.

From Clo-oose the main trail climbs again and goes along the top of a cliff where there are spectacular views, especially at sunset. Watch your footing, though. A couple of the best view spots are only about one step from a hundred-foot (30-m) drop. It is not possible to hike along the water all the way from Clo-oose, although if you are persistent, you can find a few places leading to the shore. The only easy water access is about halfway along the trail towards Whyac. Here there are petroglyphs, an old anchor on your left, blowholes and a sweeping beach to the right, as well as good campsites. A rough alternate route to Whyac starts at this point, but the main trail goes away from the water until it reaches Whyac.

At Whyac the trail bypasses an Indian village. The Indians are usually hospitable, but they have had bad experiences with hikers. On occasion their boats have been stolen or have been set adrift in the ocean. If the Indians are there they will take you across the narrows, usually for a price of $3–$5 per person. Parks Canada is endeavouring to arrange a service contract in order to guarantee that someone will be there during the summer, but in off season you should be prepared to be stranded in Whyac

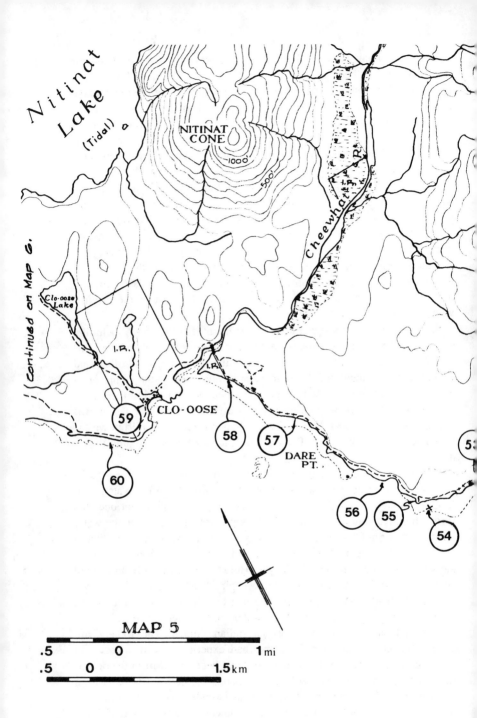

Nitinat Lake (Tidal)

NITINAT CONE

1000'

500'

Cheewhat R.

Continued on Map 6.

Clo-oose Lake

I.R.

I.R.

59

CLO-OOSE

58

57

DARE PT.

60

56

55

54

53

MAP 5

.5   0   1mi

.5   0   1.5km

34

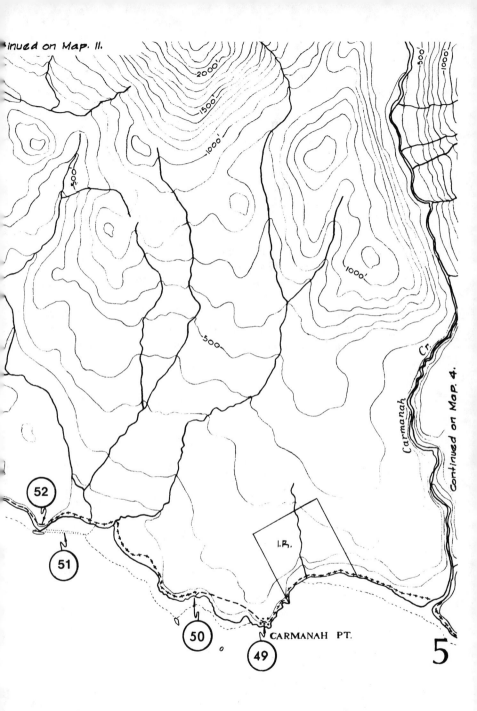

inued on Map. 11.

20000'

1500'

1000'

500'

500'

1000'

1000'

500'

Carmanah Cr.

Continued on Map. 4.

52

51

I.R.

50

49

CARMANAH PT.

5

35

[49] *Carmanah Point Lighthouse. Trail passes behind it. Please do not bother the lighthouse keepers.*

[50] *Trail from [49] joins beach. Shore route from [49] to [50] is rocky but passable at low tide.*

[51] *"The Cribs," interesting natural breakwater.*

[52] *Prominent headland. Beach route from here to [57] is passable at low tide, but trail route is easier.*

[53] *Trail rejoins beach.*

[54] *Some wreckage of the 1,600-ton steamer* Santa Rita *(wrecked in 1923) may be visible in a surge channel at low tide.*

[55] *Sea chasm and ledge block shelf. Passable at low tide. Rough trail bypasses these.*

[56] *Ladders, marked by rough sign on trail, give beach access or exit.*

[57] *Trail rejoins beach. Good camping.*

[58] *Trail leaves beach, crosses peninsula to Cheewhat suspension bridge.*

[59] *Intersection with Brown's Bay Trail, which is in very poor condition.*

[60] *Easy beach access. Petroglyphs. Blowhole and good camping to right. Anchor of barquentine* Skagit, *wrecked 1906, on shelf to left.*

for a day or two or even longer. For this reason, Parks Canada does not recommend using the southern section of the trail from October through mid-May.

Nitinat Narrows is one of the most spectacular locations on the entire west coast, and one of the most dangerous. The currents roar through at up to eight knots, creating treacherous whirlpools. The outgoing tide is especially dangerous; as it meets incoming swells, huge standing waves are formed. The only really safe time for taking a boat through the narrows is at high water slack, a period of about six minutes each day. Many drownings have occurred here. Whyac itself is a very old village, possibly one of the oldest on the west coast of North America. If you are stranded at Whyac, there is room for one tent in the trees by the beach outside the village at the entrance to the narrows, but because this is Indian land, you must get permission before camping there. An alternative place to camp is a half mile back on the beach. If you are coming from Pachena and are stranded, you might have to return to one of the long beaches. Nitinat Lake is at present the only midpoint for entering or leaving the trail. For details, see Chapter Four. If logging gets as close to the trail as present plans allow, there will be other entry points.

The portion of the trail between Nitinat Narrows and the Klanawa River is considered by many to be the most dramatically beautiful part of the West Coast Trail. It has almost everything—sweeping sandy beaches, sea caves, rocky headlands, shelves teeming with marine life, and the famous Tsusiat Falls. It can be hiked easily in a day, but deserves a more leisurely visit.

From Nitinat Narrows the trail climbs again, and you get glimpses of the sea as it surges against headlands and chasms. Between here and Tsusiat Falls there are many camping areas, but water can be a problem during the dry season. The trail rejoins the beach about a mile (1½ km) from the narrows, and from there to Tsusiat Falls you can do most of your hiking along the beach. But you will have to leave the beach to get around the headlands of Tsuquadra Point and Tsusiat Point, and certain other parts are passable only if the tide is right. Highlights are the sea caves at Tsuquadra and Tsusiat points, and Hole-in-the-Wall at Tsusiat Point. The caves are in the Tsuquadra Reserve, so respect them.

Tsusiat Falls has become a popular gathering place; during the hiking season there will probably be several parties camped here. Consequently, litter and sanitation are problems. In particular, the shallow sea caves in the Tsusiat area should not be used as latrines. You or a group member should carry a small trowel or other digging tool in order to properly dispose of your waste in the forest floor. Unfortunately, outhouses along the trail have been vandalized to such an extent that Parks Canada is reluctant to replace them. The use of nonbiodegradable soap is causing a

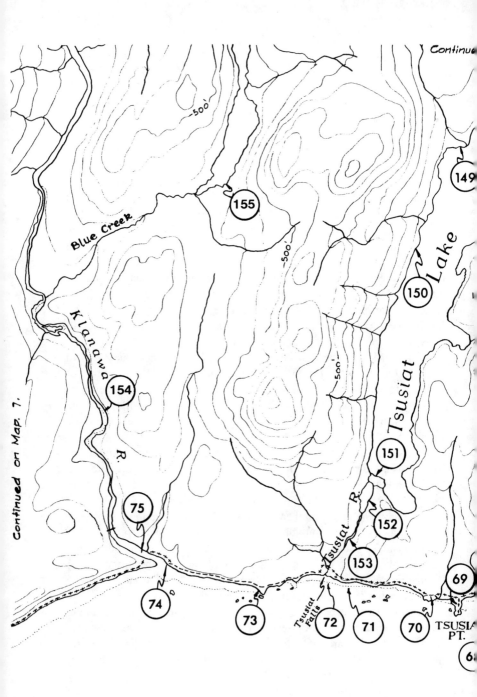

Continued on Map. 7.

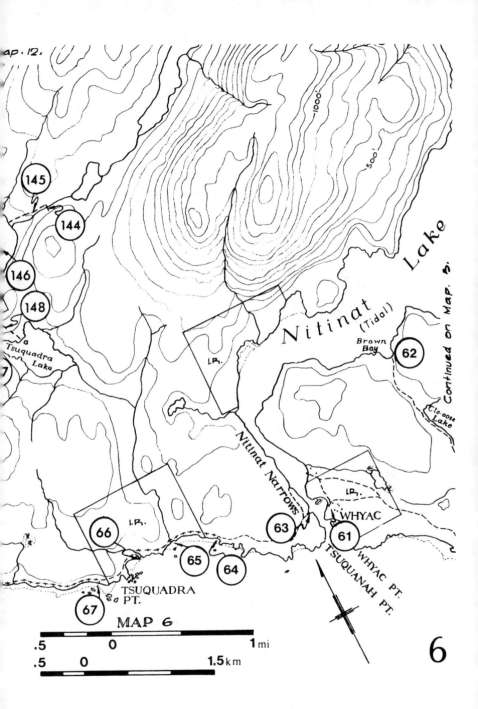

ap. 12.

145

144

146

148

Tsuquadra Lake

62

Nitinat (Tidal) Lake

Brown Bay

Clo-oose Lake

Continued on Map. 5.

Nitinat Narrows

I.R.

I.R.

I.R.

66

65

64

63

61

WHYAC

WHYAC PT.

TSUQUANAH PT.

TSUQUADRA PT.

67

MAP 6

.5   0   1 mi

.5   0   1.5 km

6

[61] *Whyac. Summer residence of some of Nitinat Band. Very dangerous channel. Charge for ferry across Nitinat Narrows usually is from $3–$5 per person. Often possible to purchase fish or crabs here.*

[62] *Brown Bay. Access to West Coast Trail from Nitinat Lake. Trail, which is in very poor condition, leaves from left of bay next to old shack.*

[63] *Trail resumes on far side of Nitinat Narrows. Take trail to your left.*

[64] *Trail joins beach.*

[65] *Excellent campsite at end of long, fine sand beach.*

[66] *Access trail to beach. Tsuquadra Point is to the west as you come out on the beach. By the point area, fantastic set of wave-worn galleries, well worth exploring. Caves are included in Tsuquadra Reserve, so respect them. Headland impassable.*

[67] *Trail rejoins beach.*

[68] *Headland dangerous at high tide. Bypass trail available.*

[69] *Tsusiat Point. Impassable at high tide. Side trail leads to Hole-in-the-Wall.*

[70] *Trail over headland. From here to Tsusiat Falls easily passable at low tide.*

[71] *Long stairway from trail down to beach near Tsusiat Falls.*

[72] *Tsusiat Falls. Excellent campsite. Some dry caves nearby. Littering is becoming a problem. Take care at top of falls; rocks are very slippery.*

[73] *Impassable headland.*

[144] *Waterfall.*

[145] *Rough trail.*

[146] *Lagoon; many crabapple trees around perimeter.*

[147] *Old trail.*

[148] *Blowdown area.*

[149, 150] *Campsites.*

[151] *Good campsite. Log jam marks creek entrance. Carry canoes over log jam.*

[152] *Little Tsusiat Lake; lots of water lilies.*

[153] *River can be waded; many deadfalls and overhangs. Canoes must be lined down and lifted over some deadfalls. When river is high, more lifting required. Trails on either side of the creek.*

[154] *Good canoe water for 2 miles (3.2 km), then rocky. After junction with Blue Creek, much logging debris.*

[155] *Blue Lake.*

problem with algal growth in the pool at the base of the falls. Drinking water should be obtained from the falls and not the pool.

Tsusiat Falls is also the joining point with the Hobiton-Tsusiat canoeing circuit, which is discussed in Chapter Three. There are now rough trails up both sides of Tsusiat Creek to Tsusiat Lake. If you do decide to walk out on the creek bed from the bridge to the edge of the falls, be extremely careful. It is very slippery, and there is a 60-foot (18.3-m) drop.

From Tsusiat Falls to the Klanawa River you are completely separated from the ocean except for one or two rough, steep access points. On the south side of the Klanawa stands a lineman's cabin which is still in fairly good condition. The cable car ride across the Klanawa is an exciting experience, but if you are alone, it will be hard on your shoulders. It is best if one person rides in the car and pulls while a partner assists from shore. The construction crews are learning about cable cars as they go, modifying and improving them by trial and error. Be sure to notify the Park Warden if the car is out of order. The Klanawa, like the Cheewhat, is tidal, so you may have to go a fair way upstream to get good water. You should also keep the tide in mind when selecting your picturesque campsite on the banks of the river.

It is possible to hike from the Klanawa to the trail's end in one day, but is not desirable to do so unless you have to meet a deadline. This is a long hike, and the scenery deserves to be enjoyed. Water is plentiful with the possible exception of the low portion for the first 2½ miles (4 km) west of the Klanawa. The trail goes mainly through the forest, but there are various spots where the beach is accessible for extended hiking. You can walk from the Klanawa to Michigan Creek on the beach, except for the section between [76] and [79]. From the Darling to the Michigan, lack of use is causing the trail to become overgrown. At last report, the trail is not maintained from Tsocowis Creek to Michigan Creek.

The famous *Valencia* wreck of 1906 occurred at Shelter Bight, about 2½ miles (4 km) west of the Klanawa River. An overview of the wreck site occurs along the trail where it skirts the cliffs through an old burn where trees are scanty just west of the donkey engine (a relic left by trail builders in 1909). Because of the inadequate rescue facilities, 126 people died, not from injuries sustained in the wreck but by drowning or exposure. The shock generated by this disaster stimulated construction of an improved lifesaving trail. It was road width to Shelter Bight, a wide trail to Carmanah, and a narrow trail from Carmanah to Port Renfrew. Over the years, the *Valencia* has sunk completely, and no remnants of wreckage are now visible.

The capstan on the rocks at Shelter Bight may have come from the four-masted steam schooner *Robert E. Lewers*, which went aground in

1923. Earlier, in 1895, the magnificent iron square-rigger *Janet Cowan* was wrecked. There is wreckage in a surge channel at the outlet of Billy Goat Creek, and at the mouth of Michigan Creek are the boiler and some smaller parts of the steam schooner *Michigan*, wrecked in 1893.

The cable car crossing at the Darling River requires extremely hard work to operate and thus it is recommended that you cross the river upstream on logs and natural bridges. The campsite at the Darling, being fairly close to Pachena, is heavily used and susceptible to damage. Hikers are urged to treat the area gently. Additional camping can be found near Tsocowis and Michigan creeks and at points between.

On a bulletin board at the entrance to the lighthouse at Pachena Point is a listing of the times that the lighthouse and grounds may be visited by the public.

The trail from Pachena Point to the end is almost a road; in fact, for many years it was the supply road for the lighthouse. The many gulleys make it harder to hike than you would expect, and it is also almost completely in the forest with few view points. You may want to try one or more of the several water access or view paths. In fall and early spring, sea lions can be seen on Flat Rocks. The camping areas on the beaches below the trail have ample water.

Just past the trail's end is an information centre staffed by Parks Canada. The centre is open 9 A.M. to 5 P.M. daily from mid-May until late September. You should sign in here, either coming or going, both for your safety and to provide records that are being compiled to help protect the West Coast Trail from other than non-recreational use.

To reach Bamfield, you must go through the parking lot to the main road. Bamfield has accommodations and supplies and is also the terminus for the Bamfield–Port Alberni ferry, *Lady Rose*.

If you want to camp at Pachena Bay, please note that most of the beach area lies within an Indian reserve. The Ohiaht Indian Band which owns the Pachena Bay Reserve operates a commercial campground. Camping is also permitted for a maximum stay of three nights on the beach near the end of the trail. Camping is not allowed on the grassy area in front of the now abandoned buildings of Camp Ross Bible Camp. Please respect the buildings as private property.

HIKING AROUND BAMFIELD

If you have to wait in Bamfield a day or two for transportation out, there are a few day hikes and short excursions worth taking. A visit to the original townsite of Bamfield on the east side of Bamfield Inlet is recommended. Getting across the inlet should not be too much of a problem, as boats go back and forth regularly. Just ask at the main dock.

The original townsite of Bamfield is much more interesting than the west side. Very few cars are seen here, and a maze of walking trails connects with the "main street"—a boardwalk along the waterfront. Short excursions can be made to Brady Beach and other beaches beyond by following the occasional sign. If you get lost, ask for directions. Brady Beach is a delightful spot for a picnic. However, there are no toilet facilities or overnight camping facilities.

Hiking to Cape Beale now requires water transportation to the bottom of Bamfield Inlet. At this writing, the Indian Reserve to the south of the original Bamfield townsite remains closed to the public. The Indians closed the reserve to prevent vandalism to some of their sacred sites. There is a water taxi service operating out of the highway side of Bamfield. Call 728-3228 for information and rates.

To reach the start of the Cape Beale trail, head for the southeast corner of the inlet. The trail begins at a marker to the east of a small creek which empties into the inlet. Proceed in a southerly direction along an unmaintained trail until you reach Kichha Lake. A rough trail branches to your right and heads west for Topaltos Bay. When you reach Topaltos Bay, hike along the beach for about two-thirds of its length to where the trail goes into the forest. The rest of the hike can be different since there are a number of broken boards in the boardwalks as well as deep mud in parts of the trail. If your goal is the Cape Beale lighthouse, you must reach the final channel at low tide, which is the only time that the channel is dry. There is no camping at the lighthouse.

Another interesting side trip is to Keeha Bay. At the "Y" at the northeast tip of Kichha Lake, take the trail to your left which goes around the lake. The trail is in very poor condition towards the southern end of the lake; you may have to bushwhack or slog through the mud to reach dry ground. Cape Beale or Pachena Bay can be reached from Keeha Bay but entails rock scrambling and some gruelling bushwhacking.

HEADLAND BETWEEN 150 YARD CREEK AND TRISLE CREEK

— 3 —
Nitinat Lakes

THE BEST APPROACH to the Nitinat Lakes is from B. C. Forest Products Company's Knob Point picnic ground on the north side of Nitinat Lake. More details are given in Chapter Four.

A word of warning is appropriate about Nitinat Lake. Firstly, it is tidal and therefore salty; secondly, it can be dangerous, with high winds. A westerly wind generally sets in about 10:00 each morning, sometimes earlier, and rapidly builds into a steep chop. To avoid paddling into this wind, set off early in the morning. If you time your trip properly, you will have the wind behind you coming back. The land at the mouth of Hobiton Creek is Indian Reserve. Although it looks deserted, it is used by the Indians in the summer and fall. Camping is not permitted on these lands without the Nitinat Band's permission.

Note the logging road high above the lake near Hobiton Creek. It represents an incident in the long battle to save these lakes from logging. The road was being pushed rapidly towards Hobiton Lake in 1971 when public pressure persuaded the provincial government to impose a moratorium on the road until the fate of the Hobiton-Tsusiat watershed was decided. There was a flurry of concern in May of 1977 when it was observed that the road was again being extended, but conservation groups were assured that it was merely going up the hill to give access to unlogged timber along the shore of Nitinat Lake and was not going into Hobiton Lake. Hopefully, the disposition of the watershed will soon be resolved.

At Hobiton Creek you will have to decide whether to portage your canoe or line it up the creek. Lining up is faster and easier, unless the water in the creek is very cold or the flow is too high or too low. Use the rapids near the mouth as a gauge: if the rocks are barely covered, the flow is probably too low; if the water is racing over them, it may be too high. Lining up the creek is fairly straightforward but will involve wading in well above the knees. The downstream half has the greater fall and is rockier. Some of the pools are quite deep and will require paddling across, which cannot be done easily if the flow is very high. It is better to line down the creek when coming out unless the water is unusually high.

Continued on Map 8.

1500'
1000'
2000'
1500'
1000'
1500'
1000'
1500'

Darling

Tsocowis

1000'
500'

500'

1000'

500'

R.

500'

80

79

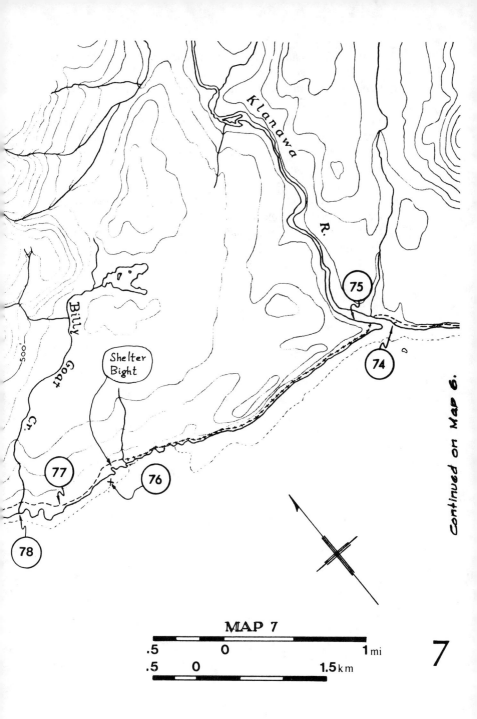

Klanawa R.

Billy Goat Cr.

Shelter Bight

500

75

74

77

76

78

Continued on Map 6.

MAP 7

.5　　　　0　　　　　　　　1 mi

.5　　0　　　　　　1.5 km

7

[74] *Trail parallels Klanawa River. Easy beach walking at low tide. Good cabin on this side of river.*

[75] *Cable car crossing. Please do not abuse it. Report malfunctions of this and other cable crossings to park warden.*

[76] *Site of the* Valencia *grounding and subsequent deaths of 126 persons. Just east of here, at Shelter Bight, is a capstan which may have come from the* Robert E. Lewers. *It is not possible to hike along the beach from Shelter Bight to [79].*

[77] *Old donkey engine.*

[78] *Wreckage of the* Janet Cowan, *grounded in 1895, may be visible in a surge channel at the mouth of Billy Goat Creek at low tide.*

[79] *Trail rejoins beach by stream. Interesting gorge about a kilometre upstream.*

Hobiton Creek is a gem; the waters are warm in summer and are always clear. It is lined by enormous trees, and along the banks there is a wide variety of flowers and shrubs which attract a rich bird life. Hobiton Creek leaves the lake at a long still pond which is also the end of the portage. At the downstream end of the pond there is a log jam. In recent years during the months of May, June and July, Fisheries officers have closed Hobiton Creek to any vessel, including canoes, to protect migrating sockeye salmon. During closed periods, it is necessary to portage around Hobiton Creek. For information on closures, contact the Government of Canada Fisheries and Oceans Department in Port Alberni.

To find the Nitinat Lake end of the portage, paddle to the south end of the Hobiton Indian Reserve, which is the logged-off area. There you will find a rock point with a large triangular marker. The beginning of the portage is in the cove beyond the point; you start by walking up a big log.

The portage is rough. Each winter new windfalls occur, and so far all clearing has been done by volunteers. (Although both provincial and federal governments have made a commitment to protect the area, agreements have still not been reached which would enable Parks Canada to officially take responsibility for maintenance.) Allow two hours for the portage, which will involve one trip with the canoe and one trip with packs — carrying both at once would be very difficult. In addition to windfalls, there are mud holes and slippery banks. A two-man carry is advisable in most cases. Footwear with good traction is essential at all portages.

From the end of the portage, there is a good view of the north shore of Hobiton Lake with its majestic sweep of huge fir, cedar, and hemlock trees and the dominating Hobiton Ridge. Most of the campsites on the lake are scattered along the north side; some of the most popular ones are shown on the map. At Dead Alder, ten or more tents can be stretched along the shore. Hitchie Creek site can take about eight tents, and there is room for several at Cedar Log. Firewood is becoming scarce. You should use a camp stove whenever possible and never cut live trees. Remember also that fish spawn in the small creek beds here, so you should avoid disturbing the gravel any more than necessary.

The flat at the mouth of Hitchie Creek has good camping, and the breeze limits insect pests. There is a spectacular waterfall part way up the creek which can be reached by the determined hiker, although it involves scrambling and wading. By scrambling out of the canyon near the falls and bushwhacking, Hitchie Lake can be reached, but this scramble is both difficult and dangerous, requiring the use of ropes, and we do not recommend it to anyone but the most experienced.

The Cedar Log campsite is at the mouth of a small creek and is marked by a large log projecting out into the water. From this campsite, it takes about an hour to climb Hobiton Ridge through the old trees. There

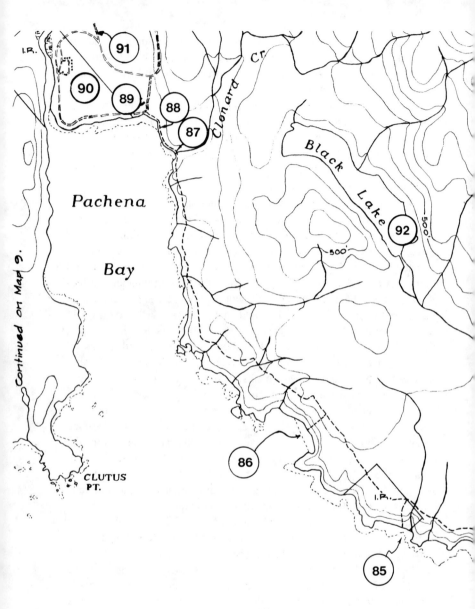

Pachena

Bay

Clonard Cr.

Black Lake

500'

500'

CLUTUS
PT.

Continued on Map 9.

I.R.

I.R.

I.R.

(91)

(90)

(89)

(88)

(87)

(92)

(86)

(85)

SEABIRD
RKS

50

1500'

1000'

1500'

1000'

1000'

1000'

500'

Darting

R.

Michigan

1000'

500'

Cr.

80

81

Continued on Map. 7.

R.

82

84   83   PACHENA PT.

MAP ☙

.5   0   1 mi

.5   0   1.5 km

8

[80] *Darling River. Small waterfall upstream. Good campsite, but sometimes crowded and littered.*

[81] *Michigan Creek. Good campsite. Wreckage here of the* Michigan, *1893.*

[82] *Pachena Point Lighthouse. Please do not bother the keepers.*

[83] *Flat Rocks Sea Lion colony, March to May; occasionally at other times.*

[84] *Unimproved beach access trail. Status of this trail is unknown.*

[85] *Unimproved beach access trail.*

[86] *Unimproved beach access trail.*

[87] *Last camping area before end of trail.*

[88] *End of West Coast Trail.*

[89] *Information booth; parking lot behind. Register for safety and to establish usage of the trail.*

[90] *Ohiaht Indian Reserve is private property.*

[91] *Road to Bamfield.*

[92] *Scenic Black Lake. Will probably be excluded from the park.*

are no trails up the ridge yet, but passage is easy as long as you avoid the gullies. The forest is open and carpeted with ferns. There is excellent swimming at both Hitchie Creek and Cedar Log campsites, where steep dropoffs occur, but inflowing creeks cool the water here.

Cedar Log camp makes a good jumping-off point for Squalicum Lake. The Squalicum trail starts at a small gravel beach on the south shore of Hobiton, about half a mile to the east of the camp. The entrance to the trail lies below a saddle in the ridge and is marked by a red ribbon. Enormous mossy trees line the trail, which rises steeply 400 feet (145 m). There are also enormous windfalls. It is not recommended to take canoes over this trail, but if you are determined you should have at least three people.

Squalicum Lake is scenic, but difficult to explore without a canoe or raft. From its western end, Squalicum Creek runs westward through two small lakes to discharge into Tsusiat Lake. The descent of this creek is extremely rough, though a few people have travelled down it with rubber rafts. There is a 30 foot (9.1 m) high waterfall about 400 yards (365 m) up from Tsusiat Lake.

The entrance to the portage between Hobiton and Tsusiat is on the south shore, a little to the east of the end of Hobiton Lake. It is marked by a large log sloping into the lake, and by tape. The portage is rough, with large deadfalls, mud holes and slippery banks. It was originally cleared by volunteers and has had nothing but volunteer labour since. Over the last few years the trail has deteriorated. You will need about one and a half hours to carry a canoe over it; with a pack, the portage takes about 45 minutes.

The portage passes beside a pretty bog lying on the crest of the ridge. Tiny sundews — insectivorous plants — can be found in the mossy sections here, making a side trip worthwhile, but we urge you to step carefully to let the ground recover. In the past, the bog was almost destroyed by the hundreds of canoe-carrying hikers who struggled through the deep mud. A bypass trail was constructed by a volunteer group from Mt. Douglas Secondary School, Victoria, and Sierra Club members. Such upgrading is to be commended, but is is rough and occasional, and we hope that the problem of trail maintenance will be solved in the near future.

As you approach Tsusiat, the trees become smaller, but the forest still remains open and easy to traverse. The exception is in the gullies and along the lake shores, which have a growth of crabapple and salal that is difficult to penetrate. The portage ends at the east end of Tsusiat Lake. Enough space has been cleared to provide camping space for a small group, but the site is boggy and cramped.

Tsusiat Lake has a very different character from that of Hobiton

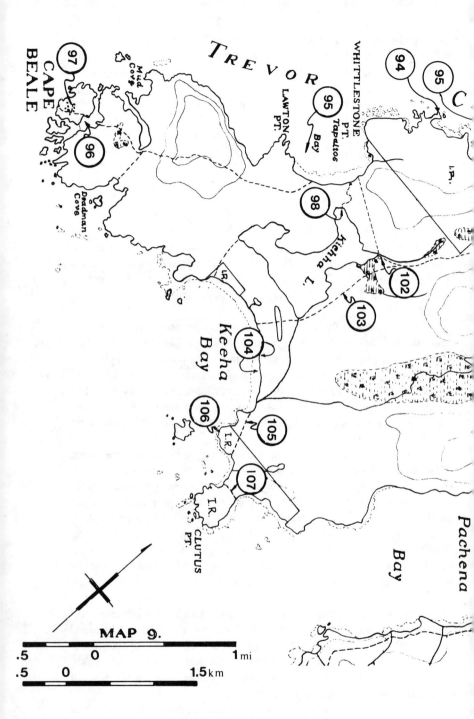

TREVOR

WHITTLESTONE PT.

LAWTON PT.

Mud Cove

97 CAPE BEALE

96

Deadman's Cove

95 Bay

PT. Tapaltos

94

95

C

I.R.

98

Kichha L.

102

103

I.R.

Keeha Bay

104

105

106

I.R.

107

I.R.

CLUTUS PT.

Pachena Bay

MAP 9.

.5   0   1 mi

.5   0   1.5 km

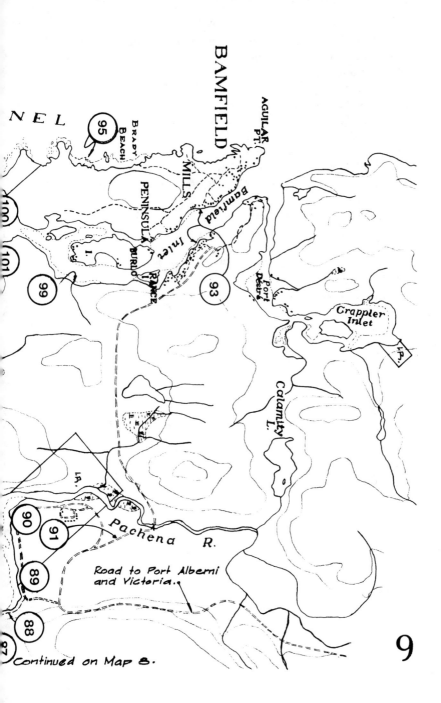

BAMFIELD

AGUILAR PT.

Bamfield

MILLS

Brady Beach

PENINSULA

BURLO

BURLO

Inlet

PRINCE

Port Desire

Crappler Inlet

I.R.

Calamity L.

Pachena R.

Road to Port Alberni
and Victoria.

N E L

95

100

101

99

93

90

91

89

88

97

Continued on Map 8.

9

55

[93] *Bamfield. The* Lady Rose *berths on both sides of the inlet. See schedule in Chapter Four.*

[94] *Execution Rock.*

[95] *Attractive bays.*

[96] *This channel dries at low tide.*

[97] *Cape Beale Lighthouse.*

[98] *Rough access trail to Kichha Lake.*

[99] *Beach walkable at low tide.*

[100] *Trail through Indian reserve now closed.*

[101] *Start of trail access to Cape Beale and Kichha Lake. Possible portage.*

[102] *Kichha Lake. Launch canoe here.*

[103] *Rough trail to Keeha Bay.*

[104] *Wide, sweeping beach.*

[105, 107] *Trails across headlands. Respect Indian Reserve lands.*

[106] *Shore route, if chosen, leads through arch. A deep pool beneath requires wading.*

Lake. Although Hobiton Ridge still dominates the view, it is now much farther away. The timber along the shores is smaller, and there are islands with interesting examples of stunted growth.

If there is no wind, it will take between one and one and a half hours to paddle to the western end of the lake. About halfway along the south shore, near a small island, you will see the narrow entrance to the lagoon. This sheltered spot was used by the Nitinat Indian Band in former times as a place of refuge when they were being harried by enemies. The lagoon is shallow and usually warm, a good place for a dip.

Some canoeists have reported a rather surprising nuisance on Tsusiat Lake, especially during June and July: the presence of large numbers of seagulls. Apparently, they are often so numerous as to be bothersome.

A trail to Tsuquadra Lake leaves from the southwest tip of the lagoon, but is very overgrown and almost impossible to find. Another trail leads from the lagoon up Squalicum Creek to the falls, but it is extremely rough.

There are not as many campsites on Tsusiat Lake as on Hobiton Lake. The ones at [149] and [150] on the map are the best. Another good area is at the west end near the log jam marking the outflow from the lake.

You will probably not want to take your canoe down Tsusiat Creek. Leave it at Little Tsusiat Lake and hike down. There are now trails on each side of the creek, the one on the south side being the better. Do not walk down the centre of the creek as it is quite fragile and already showing signs of damage from overuse.

If you wish to take your canoe down the creek to the sea, go over the log jam, move into Little Tsusiat Lake and enter the Tsusiat River, which is quite shallow. Passage on the river is slow because of the large numbers of fallen trees across it. If the river is not too high, it is possible to take canoes down to the top of Tsusiat Falls. Be very careful though; the creek bottom is slippery and the drop is 60 feet (18.3 m).

If you are an expert canoeist, you can portage the canoe about a quarter mile to the east, struggle down about seventy-five steps to the bottom, and launch your canoe through the surf. You can then paddle east to Nitinat Narrows and through to Nitinat Lake. Be warned that this is potentially very dangerous, and should be attempted only if you are a highly experienced ocean canoeist. If you miscalculate when launching into the surf, you will probably suffer only a soaking or the loss of your equipment. If you miscalculate when canoeing through Nitinat Narrows, you could lose your life, as have many others. It is only really safe at slack tide, preferably high water slack, which lasts about six minutes each day. Remember that slack water in the Narrows does not occur when the ocean tide is slack, but rather when the level of Nitinat Lake is equal to that of the ocean. At the high ocean tide there may be a very strong flow through the Narrows into the lake. You will need west coast tide and current tables.

Read them accurately, allowing for daylight saving time. And, of course, the sea must be calm enough to be canoed on. Especially avoid strong southwesterly winds. These give a strong following sea, which can cause a canoe to run out of control and collapse. Also watch for outlying shelves over which swells sometimes break suddenly. These warnings may sound exaggerated, even melodramatic, but the open ocean is not like a sheltered ocean. If you are not experienced with it, you can get into trouble very easily, and because of the strong surf, you cannot simply go ashore anywhere. If you capsize, twenty minutes in the cold ocean water could result in hypothermia and loss of consciousness. To repeat: Nitinat Narrows is extremely dangerous for inexperienced boaters.

If you have canoed from Tsusiat Falls and through Nitinat Narrows, you should not have any problems with lake turbulence. Do, however, remember the midday winds and give yourself time to pull ashore for a few hours if they get too strong. On the other hand, if the winds are not too strong, you can sail back up the lake.

In general, Hobiton Lake can be enjoyed in a two-day weekend, but to reach and explore Tsusiat Lake takes three days. If you want to reach the sea from Tsusiat, allow two days until the portages and trails are improved.

One final word. The Hobiton-Tsusiat Watershed — like other areas which get heavy use — is beginning to accumulate garbage. This unsightliness can be avoided if everyone follows the rule: "If you can take it in, you can take it out." But not everyone bothers, so we urge concerned people to help by taking out any bits of non-biodegradable garbage they find.

— 4 —
Transportation and Trail Access

TRANSPORTATION TO AND FROM the trailheads can be a bit of a logistical problem to arrange. Most parties leave a car at either end of the trail. If you do this, allow a full day for travel.

The north end of the trail has better public transportation facilities. The *Lady Rose* operates as a ferry between Bamfield and Port Alberni. At this writing the vessel leaves Port Alberni at 8:00 A.M. on Tuesdays, Thursdays and Saturdays, reaching Bamfield East Dock at 12:30 P.M.; it leaves Bamfield at 1:00, arriving at Port Alberni at 5:00 P.M. In July and August there is a Sunday run, leaving Port Alberni at 9:00 A.M. and leaving Bamfield East Dock at 12:30 P.M. and Bamfield West Dock at 3:30 P.M. Hikers should note that they must be at the East Dock by 12:30 P.M. in order to guarantee their boarding.

At this writing there is also a bus service, The Pachena Bay Express which operates between Port Alberni and Bamfield. The bus will pick up hikers from the trailhead at Pachena Bay in the mornings on Mondays, Wednesdays, Fridays and Sundays in the summer. The bus arrives in Port Alberni in the afternoon. For up-to-date information on times and fares, contact the Parks Canada Information Centre at 728-3234.

No other routes have public transportation on a regular basis. They require the use of logging roads established by the forest companies and are subject to various restrictions. With the exception of the road from Mesachie Lake to Port Renfrew and the one from Nanaimo to Nitinat Lake, the main roads are now open to the public 24 hours a day, but loaded logging trucks still have the right of way. The two exceptions are only open during non-working hours, which usually means from 6:00 P.M. to 6:00 A.M. on weekdays and all day on weekends. No overnight camping is allowed on company administered forest land except at designated camping sites.

(Continued on Map 12.)

I.R.

115

114

108

N I T I N A T   L A K

(T i d a l)

124

C

Continued on Map 11.

MT. ROSANDER

500'
1000'
1500'
1000'
1500'
1000'
500'
500'
1500'
1000'
1500'
2000'
2500'
3000'
500'
1000'
1500'

110

113

09

112

111

I.R.

I.R.

I.R.

I.R.

I.R.

Road from
Victoria & Port Alberni

Campus Cr.

HOUSE RIVER

1500'

2000'

1500'

500'

1000'

1500'

MAP 10

.5   0   1 mi

.5   0   1.5 km

10

61

[108] *B. C. Forest Products Knob Point picnic grounds and boat launch.*

[109] *MacMillan Bloedel and B. C. Forest Service campground.*

[110] *Nitinat River. Good canoeing water up to Nitinat Falls. Beware of standing waves at mouth when Nitinat Lake is rough.*

[111] *Village of Nitinat Indian Band. Possible boat trips down Nitinat Lake.*

[112] *Sandy beach and driftwood.*

[113] *Road to Knob Point.*

[114] *BCFP road, originally headed for Hobiton Lake. Now used for logging along Nitinat Lake.*

[115] *Hobiton Indian Reserve, identified by old clear-cut. Good beach. Respect privacy and property.*

Although the logging companies claim that these roads are private, this is so only where they cross private land. For the safety of everyone, co-operation on travel restrictions is essential, especially on the spur logging roads. But do not let yourself be harassed into thinking that you have no right to be on the roads.

Access to Port Renfrew can be made from Victoria by way of Sooke and Jordan River, including about 15 miles (24 km) of unpaved road, and from Duncan by way of Shawnigan Lake and the San Juan Valley road, including 25 miles (40 km) of unpaved road, which is only suitable for travel with 4WD vehicles. An alternative from Duncan is via Mesachie Lake, though this is no shorter and travel is restricted to non-working hours. There are limited hotel and motel accommodations in Port Renfrew. Good camping is found on the long beach at the head of Port San Juan, where you will be within a few minutes' walk of the Pacheenaht Reserve. You will need to cross the Gordon River to the beginning of the trail. The usual fare for this boat trip is $3 per person. Longer trips to Thrasher Cove, Owen Point or Camper Bay are also available at the rates of $15, $20 or $35 per trip respectively. Contact the Pacheenaht Band members or the following people in Port Renfrew: Norm Smith (647-5430) or Frank Elliott (647-5405).

From mid-May to the end of September, an Information Centre is staffed by Parks Canada employees in Port Renfrew (phone 647-5434). The centre is open from 9 A.M. until 5 P.M., and it is located on Parkinson Road next to the Recreation Centre. Hikers are encouraged to register in prior to starting out on the trail.

To use the Nitinat Lakes or to reach the trail at its mid-point, access must be via the head of Nitinat Lake. From Victoria drive through Duncan to Lake Cowichan, turn right to Youbou (the end of the blacktop), follow the north shore around the lake, turning left at the sign for Caycuse (do not go to the Crown Zellerbach Nitinat Camp). After crossing the divide, you will drop down into the Nitinat Valley and eventually come to a major T-junction, from which point looking right you can see a new bridge over the Nitinat River. The right-hand road goes to the west shore of Nitinat Lake, and on to Bamfield and Port Alberni. The left-hand road leads to the east shore of Nitinat Lake, to the Indian village at the head of the lake, and to a developed campsite. (An alternative route from Lake Cowichan, going left through Mesachie Lake, Honeymoon Bay and Caycuse, is easy to follow but is a slightly longer drive.)

If you require boat transportation to the mouth of Nitinat Lake, turn left at the T-junction, go past a sign marked "Carmanah Main," and take the next left to the Nininat Band Reserve, where someone will usually ferry you down the lake. The fee is negotiable. You should check with the band in advance by radiotelephone via Campbell River Radio, using call

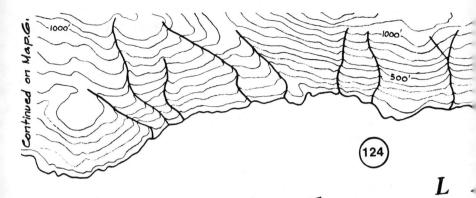

Continued on Map.G.

-1000'

-1000'

500'

(124)

N I T I N A T   L

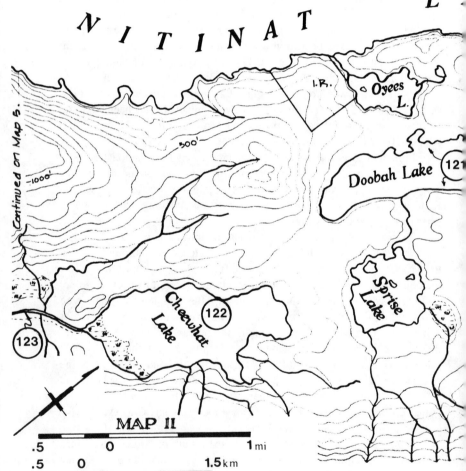

Continued on Map 5.

I.R.

Oyees L.

500'

-1000'

Doobah Lake

(121

Sprise Lake

Cheewhat Lake

(122)

(123)

MAP II

.5   0   1 mi

.5   0   1.5 km

64

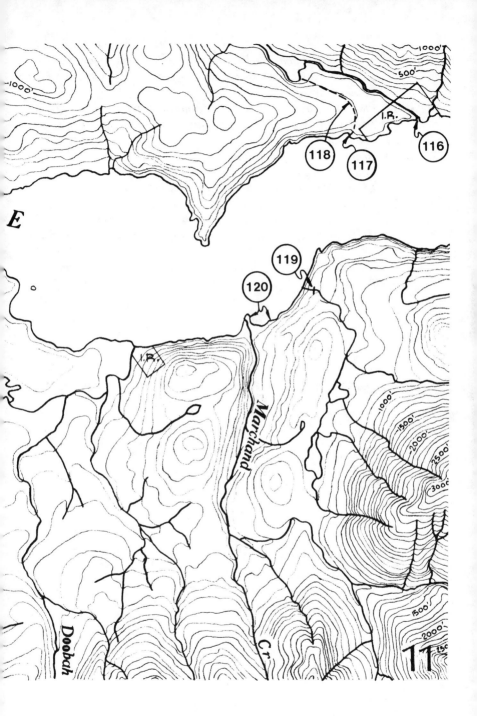

E

I.R.

118 117 116

119

120

I.R.

Marchand

Doobah

Cr

11

[116]   *Mouth of Hobiton Creek. If Indians are salmon fishing, use portage. Creek is often closed during the sockeye migration, mid-May through July.*

[117]   *Start of portage in cove to west of point having triangular marker.*

[118]   *Portage trail rough. Allow about an hour for carrying canoe.*

[119]   *Waterfall.*

[120]   *Beaches suitable for camping.*

[121]   *Much logging around these rarely visited lakes.*

[122]   *Cheewhat Lake is wintering area for trumpeter swans.*

[123]   *Salmon run in Cheewhat all year round.*

[124]   *Caution! Keep close to shore on Nitinat Lake. Winds get up suddenly and are predominantly westerly after 10:00 A. M.; sometimes earlier. Nitinat Lake is cold; if your canoe tips, you will suffer from exposure. Also full of jellyfish in some seasons. Seals and otters can be seen.*

sign N692932. Otherwise, there is no regular transportation down the lake. If you have your own boat, or if you are looking for an attractively developed campground, continue past the Indian village to a campsite developed by MacMillan Bloedel and the B.C. Forest Service on the shores of the lake. It has a boat launching ramp and a place to leave your car, at your own risk.

If you wish to canoe down Nitinat Lake or canoe to Hobiton and Tsusiat lakes, it is better to turn right at the T-junction, cross the bridge, make a loop around to the west side of the lake, and turn left at the Nitinat Hatchery sign. As a general guide, keep turning left after you cross the bridge. In about a mile, a sign indicates the road to Knob Point picnic ground, which is about 6 miles (10 km) along the lake shore. This site is a better start for Hobiton because it lessens the time required on Nitinat Lake and avoids having to paddle across the lake. The logging road past Knob Point continues almost to Hobiton Creek and then up the hill but does not provide easy access to Hobiton Lake. Do not forget that Nitinat Lake has dangerous midday winds.

There is a dock operated by Parks Canada during the summer at the mouth of Nitinat Lake. The dock should be kept clear. If you have a large boat, it may be either anchored or pulled above the high water mark; remember that Nitinat Lake has tides. There is safe anchorage at Brown Bay. The other usual route to the head of Nitinat Lake is from Port Alberni, along MacMillan Bloedel roads posted for Bamfield. Continue through Franklin River and follow the main road to Nitinat Lake. Another route to Bamfield, from Victoria or Duncan, takes you via the Lake Cowichan route as described. At the T-junction, turn right over the Nitinat River bridge, then continue to Franklin Camp and follow the signs to Bamfield. Using the Port Alberni approach, follow signs to Franklin and then to Bamfield. Logging road travel is fairly slow; allow about five hours from Victoria to Bamfield and about three hours from Port Alberni to Bamfield.

Access to the northern end of the West Coast Trail starts about 3 miles (5 km) before Bamfield, along a short branch to the left of the main road. If you come to a bridge over the Pachena River, you have missed the turn. There is a large parking lot. Be sure to park your car in the designated area and register at the Pachena Bay information centre.

The information centre at trailhead is open 9 to 5 from mid-May to the end of September (728-3234). Bamfield has two grocery stores, a coffee shop and a motel. There is also a first aid station across the inlet and, in season, the park warden's station is staffed (728-3244).

For up-to-date information on the trail, call the Pacific Rim National Park head office in Ucluelet (726-7721) or write Parks Canada, Box 280, Ucluelet, B.C.—the only year-round information source.

MOUTH OF HITCHIE CREEK

— 5 —
Pointers

EVEN UNDER THE MOST ADVERSE conditions, hiking the West Coast Trail can be an enjoyable experience—if you are properly prepared. On the other hand, lack of proper equipment can turn an otherwise pleasurable hike into a nightmare. So prepare for the worst, and be forewarned that on Vancouver Island's west coast the worst may be beyond anything you have ever experienced. Cold winds and torrential rains, slippery logs and muddy paths, blisters, fogged glasses, and wet clothes and sleeping bags can add up to total misery. Fortunately, most of the bad weather occurs in winter, but summer hikers should expect rain at least every second day and, if it is warm and wet, mosquitoes. The prepared hiker will avoid the additional misery of the unexpected.

Most hikers carry packs weighing between 35 and 55 pounds, although monsters of 75 pounds or more are seen. Forty pounds of equipment and food if wisely chosen will provision a person for ten days.

Four categories of equipment are needed to hike the West Coast Trail: general (the hardware necessary to protect you); clothing; cooking and eating equipment, and miscellaneous items. The following lists are intended only as a guide, and apply equally to men and women.

GENERAL EQUIPMENT

    pack (waterproof, with hip belt and side pockets)
    tent (waterproof or with waterproof fly)
    sleeping bag (synthetic fill preferred to down)
    ground sheet (optional but handy on soggy ground)
    fire starting devices
    knife
    repair materials (for clothes, tent and pack)
    50 feet of ½″ synthetic rope per couple
    tide tables
    flashlight and spare batteries (don't forget the spares)
    candles (for light and fire starting)
    compass (essential if you plan to leave the trail at any point)

watch
maps
toiletries
first aid kit (essential)
insect repellent
day pack (optional)

Sharing some of the above items within a group can lighten the individual loads and be economical. Certainly, eight people can share tents, but it would be foolish for eight people to depend on only 50 feet of rope. If the group plans to split up, each group should have a full set of equipment.

There are many types of backpacks on the market. You should compare them and consult a qualified advisor before buying one. The same applies to tents and sleeping bags. Sleeping bags filled with synthetic materials are better than down-filled bags for the weather conditions you are likely to encounter on the trail since they absorb less moisture and dry more quickly. Your sleeping bag should be light, quick-drying and effective to approximately 0°C.

Matches should be waterproofed with wax and stored in a dry place in your pack. (Safety matches are useless.) A flint can be carried, but you should also have chemical firestarter or a candle to spark it onto in case all available wood is wet; and you should carry a spare flint. Firestarter (either liquid or the solid white product) is essential, since much of the wood along the trail is either wet or green, but candle stubs are adequate substitutes. Place a candle stub under a teepee of kindling and let it burn until the wood catches. (Newsprint absorbs moisture and adds unnecessary weight to your pack.)

A small kit with needles and thread is useful for repairing cloth. For pack repair, take a few feet of thin flexible wire and some lightweight pliers. Heavy string has a variety of uses, including spare boot laces. "Duct tape" will stick to almost anything and consequently will hold anything together. Plastic bags are useful for storing items in your pack as well as keeping your matches and toilet paper dry. A flashlight with spare batteries is essential, especially in late summer and fall when the nights get longer. (The west coast forest is very dark at night.) Candles are good for reading in tents for short periods of time.

Many hikers use three contoured maps on a scale of 2 inches per mile; they are slightly more detailed than those in this book. There is also a new map, at 1¼ inches to the mile, printed on plastic, which gives the basic details very concisely. For details of forest cover and geography, there is a set of four aerial photo mosaics at 4 inches per mile. These are all available from the Map Production Division, Department of the

Environment, Parliament Buildings, Victoria, B.C., or from Map and Air Photo Sales, 553 Superior Street, Victoria, B.C.

Toiletries are considered a luxury by some hikers and a necessity by others. Toilet paper has a variety of uses. Pocket first aid kits can be purchased, or the components can be assembled.

Mosquito repellent will be needed in warm, wet weather—the liquid variety is light in weight. Garlic is rumoured to be a good insect repellent. Another solution to the problem is to camp in open areas where the wind blows the pests away. Tents with netting are useful during mosquito season.

A light day pack is handy if you plan to establish a base camp and take day trips from it.

Clothing should be chosen for warmth, weight and usefulness. Some people like to put on a set of clean clothes every morning, whereas others prefer to wear the same clothes every day, leaving room in their pack for such items as cameras or canned bacon.

CLOTHING

> boots (waterproofed, with vibram or caulked soles)
> socks (two or three pairs)
> pants (preferably wool)
> waterproof outerwear, including a hat (especially if you wear glasses)
> shorts (or a second pair of pants)
> underwear (two sets)
> shirts (at least two)
> sweater
> warm jacket
> gloves (optional during the warm months)

Vibram soles are probably best for the many types of terrain that you will encounter. Boots should be well broken in and waterproofed with wax or dubbin before you start. Like sleeping bags, footgear is usually worth what you pay for it, and a few dollars more might make the difference between pleasant hiking and blistered misery. Many hikers carry along a pair of runners which are generally more comfortable for sandy beach hiking and the easier stretches of trail.

The proper socks can help prevent blisters. Wearing a thin pair of nylon, polypropolene or olefin socks inside a pair of thick wool socks cuts down on chafing. You should carry at least one spare pair.

Jeans are fine for dry weather hiking, but when wet they act like a wick, the water working its way up your legs. Heavy wool pants are probably best. Some hikers wear shorts, rain or shine, and save their dry trousers for the campsite.

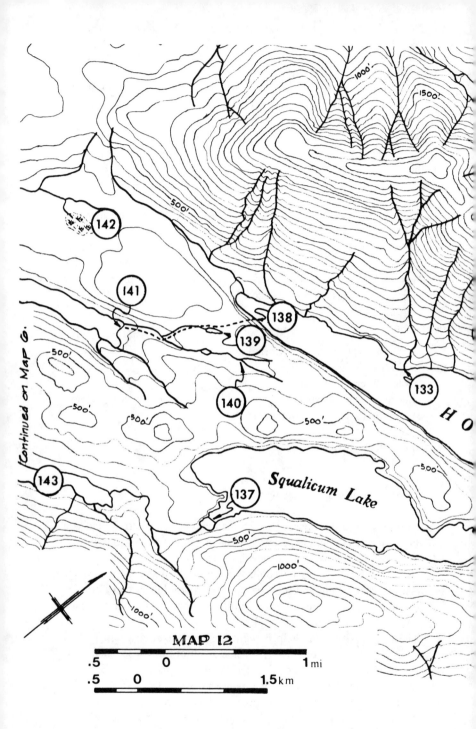

142

141

138

139

133

140

H O

500'

500'

500'

500'

500'

500'

143

137

Squalicum Lake

500'

1000'

1000'

Continued on Map G.

MAP 12

.5   0   1 mi

.5   0   1.5 km

136

ON LAKE

132

134

131

129

128

127

126

130

125

Hitchie Lake

Continued on Map 10

12

73

[125] *Pools in upper reaches of Hobiton Creek.*

[126] *Dead Alder campsite. Room for several tents when water level is low.*

[127] *Hitchie Creek campsite.*

[128] *Canyon.*

[129] *Waterfall.*

[130] *Boundary of initial logging planned by* BCFP. *Now cancelled.*

[131, 132] *Good campsites.*

[133] *Cedar Log campsite.*

[134] *Trail to Squalicum Lake, steep and rough; start marked by tape.*

[135] *Forest open. Easy going on ridges; magnificent trees.*

[136] *Hobiton Ridge.*

[137] *Log jam.*

[138] *Portage entrance on sloping log, marked by tape. Portage rough because of mud holes and much deadfall.*

[139] *Sphagnum bog. Good place to see flowers, including sundews. Bypass trail now exists.*

[140] *Gorge.*

[141] *Limited campsite, poor and boggy.*

[142] *Swamps.*

[143] *Little Squalicum Lake.*

Some form of rain gear is essential. Rainsuits of nylon or plastic are light but not very durable; rubber suits are stronger but heavy. Goretex raingear has the advantage of breathing and thus causing less perspiration. A poncho is lightweight and will cover both you and your pack but is not as effective as a suit. A hat made of terry cloth is convenient; it can be wrung out when wet and doubles as a towel. If you wear glasses, some form of peak over them is necessary.

The principle of layering is useful in this variable climate. Wearing several layers of moderately warm, lighter clothing instead of one or two layers of heavy clothing allows you to take off or put on as weather conditions change.

COOKING/EATING UTENSILS

frying pan (teflon-lined aluminum with lid)
pot lifter
pot (one gallon capacity, with lid)
pot (small with lid, or small kettle)
cup
plate
bowl
fork and spoon
knife (a general purpose knife will do for food and trail use)
can opener (if canned goods are taken)
small gas stove
fuel container
plastic garbage bags and foil (but do not forget to pack them out)
scrubber and biodegradable soap
water bottle

Heavier frying pans cook better meals, but if your pack is at a weight where every ounce counts, a lighter pan will do. The lid keeps ashes out of the food and teflon makes the pan easy to clean in cold, soapless water. A fork or spoon can double for a spatula (except with fresh eggs).

The large pot is useful for group cooking since it accommodates porridge, rice and noodles. The small pot is good for quick boiling (tea, coffee, soup, etc.).

For environmental reasons we recommend the use of backpacking-size gas stoves. They are easy to use, produce little smoke, and do not consume wood, which is in increasingly short supply. Stoves that use some form of liquid gas, such as white gas or alcohol, are preferable. A built-in pump is worth the small extra weight and a wind guard is highly desirable. Pressurized disposable cylinders are a garbage problem. If your stove requires them, pack them out.

Planning and ingenuity will help you produce satisfying, economical meals on the trail. Another approach to mealtime is to purchase freeze-dried foods, which are convenient, tasty and expensive. Most people supplement their own preparations with some freeze-dried packages. Remember to carry foil out with you. Zip-lock plastic bags are very useful for prepackaging meals and food items.

MISCELLANEOUS EQUIPMENT

What you take besides necessities depends on your experience, strength, pack size and interests. If you have a camera fetish and leave your camera at home, you could spend seven days kicking yourself for missing all those once-in-a-lifetime shots. If you are a philosopher or a poet, take along pencil and paper. (Pens tend to malfunction.) If you like to read, take along a book, especially one on hiking or wilderness foods. A deck of cards is a good device for keeping groups together. Inveterate fisherfolk will want to pack a fishing rod; a compact spincasting rig is most suitable. If you fish, don't forget that the southern banks of the Gordon and Nitinat rivers are Indian Reserves. Once the trail becomes part of the federal parks system, you will need a fishing licence.

Most of your pack's weight and bulk will be taken up by equipment. Pack weight can be cut down drastically if, before setting out, groups work out arrangements for sharing essential items.

FOOD

Food should be taken on a group basis to avoid everyone's carrying small items (such as salt, sugar, tea, etc.) that are bulky when packaged individually. Sharing foods also has the advantage of increasing group identity, a desirable reinforcement during seven days of close living. Food selection should favour high energy and low weight. Dried foods are ideal and starches are a necessity. Meat is difficult to store. Following is a suggested list:

    roast (beef or boneless ham)
    salami
    dried meat such as shrimp
    dried peas (or other vegetables)
    dried soups
    wild plants (if you are familiar with them)
    rice
    noodles
    instant potatoes

heavy bread (rye or pumpernickel)
porridge
margarine (butter will spoil)
sugar
juice crystals
coffee/tea
eggs (fresh or powdered)
canned bacon (if ham is not taken)
cheese
gorp (trail mix)
fruit (fresh and dried)
sauces, seasonings, spices
pancake mix

A ham roast is a good choice of meat as it can be used for any meal. If stored in plastic, it will spoil quickly; wrap it in waxed paper and several layers of thick brown paper. A smoked ham will keep at least seven days. Salami (whole) keeps well and combines with cheese for a quick lunch. It can also be used as a bacon substitute or added to spaghetti sauce.

Dried meats are lightweight and easy to prepare. Chinese grocery stores carry many kinds of dried food. Dried soups can be made quickly and are amenable to additions such as ham bits or wild plants. Rice, especially brown rice, is nourishing, filling and adaptable. Noodles combine well with ready-made sauces and cheese.

Bread should be a heavy variety so that it will not break up in the pack. Porridge provides a warm, hearty start to the day and is simple to prepare. Juice in the form of crystals added to water gives a psychological lift to the morning meal. Fresh eggs are difficult to pack without breaking but are sometimes worth the effort. Canned bacon is a luxury which the group can indulge in one morning.

Coffee, tea and cocoa are valuable sources of warmth and energy on cold, damp days, especially when sugar is added. An interesting combination, which be prepared in advance, is one of powdered coffee, powdered chocolate, powdered milk and brown sugar. Powdered milk can be sprinkled directly on cereal, but if you don't like milk in your tea, take along a lemon and add a few drops, as the Russians do.

Trail mix or gorp (Good Old Raisins and Peanuts) is a mixture of chocolate chips, raisins, salted peanuts and anything else which strikes your fancy. It is an excellent source of energy.

Sauces, seasonings and spices can make bland trail food worth eating. Be sure to include such items as salt, pepper, garlic, mixed spices, soy sauce, tomato sauce, gravy.

Since most food preparation will depend on water, it should be noted that there is an increasing problem with the quality of water from streams and creeks along the trail. The presence of *Ghiardia*, a micro-organism which causes stomach cramps and diarrhea, is suspected in some of the streams. Thus it is recommended that drinking water be boiled or purified through filtration. In particular, the slow-moving trickles in the bogs probably have high bacteria counts and drinking this water could cause diarrhea. The problem with water quality is compounded in arid summer. Some of the water bodies such as Nitinat, Cheewhat, Klanawa and Walbran are partially salt water and unsuitable for drinking. Boiling brackish water does not purify it but rather makes it more saline. But be sure to take water you intend to use for drinking or cooking from a spot far upstream from areas disturbed by man or animal.

— 6 —
Flora and Fauna

THERE ARE FOUR MAIN SPECIES of big trees along the West Coast Trail: Douglas-fir, western hemlock, western red cedar and Sitka spruce. Douglas-fir, *Pseudotsuga menziesii,* is found throughout British Columbia in climates ranging from very wet to fairly dry. These trees thrive on the coast, growing to enormous size, and are long-lived, some being more than 1,000 years of age. Look for Douglas-fir in younger, more open forests. They are distinguished by cones having three-pronged bracts; mature trees show thick, ridged bark. Away from the exposed coast, western hemlock, *Tsuga heterophylla,* and western red cedar, *Thuja plicata,* are the dominant trees. Hemlock is distinguished by a drooping tip. It has more graceful boughs, finer needles and less furrowed bark than Douglas-fir. The bark of the red cedar is ropy and was used extensively by the Coast Indians, as was the whole tree. Cedar burns well even when wet. Sitka spruce, *Picea sitchensis*, is a coastal tree, dominant along the west coast shore. It is identified by scaly bark and hard, sharp needles. Some pine grows along the coast in areas which lack good ground water. In young forest or in openings in the mature forest along lakes, rivers or rock outcrops, deciduous trees are more common, especially alder and maple.

The understory is too diverse to describe here. It is thickest in the open areas, sparser in the dark, mature forest areas. Salal is the most common west coast shrub; it ranges from low cover to impenetrable jungle, sometimes growing to a height of 8 feet. Salmonberry is also thick in many areas. Ferns are found, especially in shaded, damp forest and on moist banks. Huckleberry, thimbleberry and wild blackberry abound and all are edible. Many types of mushrooms grow along the trail, some of which are edible, but the hiker is advised to know a plant before sampling it.

A great variety of seaweed is visible in the ocean at low tide. One remarkable species is the sea palm, *Postelsia,* which clings to the rocks at the most turbulent part of the low tide zone. It is an impressive sight to watch the sea palm bend under the impact of huge breakers, then spring back intact after the wave has passed.

Not many large animals are seen along the trail or in the Nitinat Lakes region because forest and bush provide good cover. But deer, elk, bear and cougar have been reported in the area. Sea lions are often seen on rocks near Pachena, and seals and otters are common in Nitinat Lake.

Small animals, though, can cause you anguish: mice and mink are inveterate robbers of packs left on the ground overnight. To avoid loss and food spoilage, hang food packs every night. Many campsites have a resident mink. These animals are often quite tame through lack of contact with man. Try to keep them that way.

Bird life is rich: eagles are common and so are aquatic birds such as loons, mergansers and ducks. The now rare trumpeter swan winters on the marshes of the Cheewhat and can be seen from late fall to early spring.

Sea fishing can be rewarding along the coast, but there are also fish, especially trout, in the lakes and streams. The best fishing is at the mouth of creeks and at Nitinat Narrows. Salmon—sockeye, chum and spring—run into Hobiton Lake. Interestingly, the fish in this system spawn in gravel along the lake perimeter, particularly at the mouths of creeks rather than in stream beds. If you are in the area in the fall, consider this fact when choosing your campsite. Sockeye run into the Cheewhat system. This race is unusual because the spawners return throughout the year rather than in a concerted rush, a fact that was obviously of great importance to early Indian settlements.

Hikers are reminded that they will need a federal fishing licence for salt water sport fishing or a provincial fishing licence for fresh water fishing. When the trail and the lakes in the Nitinat Triangle become a part of Pacific Rim National Park, a National Parks fishing licence may be required.

The chum fishery of the Doobah was the richest on the coast until eliminated by early overfishing and by the crude logging practices of subcontractors to B.C. Forest Products, which filled the stream bed with debris and scoured the gravel, destroying the beauty along with the fish.

Shellfish, especially mussels, make good eating. It should be noted, though, that during the summer there can be a so-called red tide which may or may not visibly stain the water red. Eating filter-feeding molluscs during a red tide can result in a potentially fatal disease called paralytic shellfish poisoning (PSP). If there is a notice at the end of the trail of a Fisheries shellfish closure, leave these filter-feeding shellfish alone. Even if you have seen no notice, you should still eat bivalve molluscs with caution. Start with a small sampling: a tingling sensation in your lips, tongue or extremities is a danger sign. When the West Coast Trail officially becomes part of the National Parks system, taking of all wildlife including shellfish and crab will be prohibited.

Remember that conservation extends to all resources and that any species can be depleted. Never take more than your share.

— 7 —
Indian Lands

THREE SEPARATE GROUPS of Indians live along the West Coast Trail: the Pacheenaht Band at Port Renfrew; the Nitinat Band in the Nitinat Basin, and the Ohiat Band at Pachena Bay and around Cape Beale.

These Bands have several reserves along the trail and near the lakes; some are inhabited — Port Renfrew, Clo-oose, Whyac, Hobiton River, Pachena Bay, and around Nitinat Lake — and some not. All the reserve lands are clearly marked on the maps. Some reserves are only inhabited seasonally; consequently, do not assume that if no one is there the buildings have been abandoned and you have licence to enter them or to use their utensils. Remember that the reserves are private land. Even though the trail may cross the reserves, your use of it is only through the courtesy of the Indians. Your rights do not include camping on the reserve lands or use of their wood, unless you have obtained consent from Band members.

Some of the reserves carry traces of very early settlement. These must be treated with special respect and must not be interfered with, for they are of particular importance to the Bands.

Remember also that all hikers along the trail are dependent on the Indians at Port Renfrew and Whyac for ferry services, and the future success of park status for the trail depends on the willing co-operation of the Bands. Therefore, please respect their lands and property and advise other hikers, who may be unaware of the status of reserve lands, to do the same.

A CABLE CAR CROSSING

— 8 —
Special Advice

NOW THAT YOUR PACK IS FULL, you are almost ready to start your hike. But there is more to a hike than maps and boots. Six days — the average time needed to hike the West Coast Trail — may seem like a short period in the city, but on the trail where you often will not see anyone but your own party for a day or two, six days can be a long time. Generally, a near-wilderness situation requires learning a new set of attitudes.

People often find that they are being annoyed by small things that otherwise would not bother them. For instance, perhaps your best friend has a habit of whistling off key. You may never have noticed this before, but after several days of continual contact, you begin to think that your friend is doing this just to bother you.

Then there is the question of group size. Three should be considered the minimum: if a hiker is injured, one person can go for help while the other stays to look after the injured person. But a group of three sometimes has difficulty remaining on friendly terms and tends to split into two good friends and a third person. Naturally, the third person feels left out and lonely. Feeling lonely in the wilderness is more intense than loneliness elsewhere, and it often generates irrational actions. Since groups of five or six will often break up anyway, and larger groups might have trouble finding good camping spots, four is perhaps an ideal size.

You will also learn about your physical capability. If you are not a regular hiker, you could be pleasantly surprised by your stamina and inner courage. Or you could discover that your niche in life is behind a desk. But you should remember that the purpose of the hike is not to see how quickly you can reach the other end of the trail. If there are some members of your group who want to pretend they are hares, let them go to the front. More often than not the slow steady hikers finish the trail in one piece, having enjoyed the entire trip. On the other hand, dawdling should not be encouraged. You could straggle in after everyone else has had dinner, the campfire is out, and all the comfortable camping spots are gone. Another reason for not moving too slowly is that when you cross logs, your chances of falling increase with the amount of time spent standing on them.

Crossing rivers requires a special technique. If they are fast flowing, a stave is essential for maintaining balance. If there is a possibility of being swept away, use ropes and send one hiker across at a time. If everyone moves into the water at once, and one person falls, you all could be swept out to sea.

Probably the greatest danger to poorly equipped and inexperienced hikers is hypothermia, a term which literally means "too low a temperature." It can occur especially when dampness is combined with cold, a situation for which the west coast is well known, even in midsummer. A person can get so cold that the body's normal temperature control mechanisms, such as blood vessel contraction, shivering, and fast respiration, fail. At this point one's presence of mind also fails and one does not take the drastic action necessary to restore body heat. An early symptom is prolonged shivering. The later, more serious symptoms are connected with the loss of self-control — poor muscle co-ordination, weakness, slurred speech and impaired judgement. From here it is downhill to coma and death, unless appropriate action is quickly taken.

The best treatment for hypothermia is prevention: being equipped with adequate rain gear and warm clothing. If hypothermia does occur, rescuers must remember one important fact: a person with hypothermia has lost the ability to generate body heat and must be supplied with heat from an external source. This could be the warmth of a campfire, or gently inhaled steam, or warm (not hot) liquids, or of your body against that of the patient. Merely wrapping a person in warm clothing or even in a sleeping bag may be useless and can actually keep heat away. This innocent mistake has cost lives in the past.

In several places we have referred to tides. You can get a general idea by using Tofino tide tables (Tofino is the nearest reference port). These times will differ by up to half an hour from those of the West Coast Trail; heights will vary by a foot or more. Remember that times are given in standard time; add an hour for daylight saving time.

If tide prediction is critical (as in paddling through Nitinat Narrows or hiking a stretch of coast where you could be trapped by an incoming tide), you must interpolate from reference ports to secondary ports — in this case, Bamfield or Port Renfrew. These details are found in Canadian Tide and Current Tables, vol. 6, available from most marine retail outlets. This publication also gives current tables for Nitinat Bar (Nitinat Narrows).

Remember that tide and current tables are only predictions, and various circumstances can cause them to err. Do not stake your life on their absolute accuracy.

A final note: dogs are not officially encouraged on the trail.

— 9 —
Conservation

VANCOUVER ISLAND IS THE FIRST place in British Columbia where the myth of inexhaustible plenty has been completely unmasked; we know we must secure adequate protection for recreation lands on the Island before it is too late.

In the 1950s, when Justice Sloan chaired his two Royal Commissions of Enquiry into the Forest Industry, his main conclusion was that the Crown forests should be managed on a basis of sustained yield. To implement this program, the Forest Service, who were too short of funds and staff to administer all the lands directly, established many areas as tree farms which were then leased to various major logging companies. In this way, virtually all the public forest land on Vancouver Island was committed to forestry and very little attention was paid to the need for future recreation land. Essentially, the present park system on the Island is all we will ever have unless we can persuade the government to take some areas presently committed to forestry and turn them over to recreation.

In this regard the Nitinat Lakes and the West Coast Trail form an important precedent. When the Pacific Rim National Park was created in 1969, the boundaries of the trail were provisionally set at a narrow half-mile-wide strip except for enlargements at Cape Beale and Clo-oose. The original agreement between the federal and provincial authorities required that final boundaries be established before April 1974.

The tentative boundaries were inadequate to protect the character of the trail and omitted the Nitinat Lakes, an area of exceptional recreation potential and scientific interest, as well as other attractive areas such as Black Lake and the lower reaches of the Klanawa. This mistake was recognized by the National Parks Branch in April 1970 when they requested of the province that Nitinat Lakes be included in the National Park. The province, prodded by MacMillan Bloedel and B. C. Forest Products, the holders of Tree Farm Licences 21 and 27 in the area, balked. This was the beginning of conflict between logging companies and conservationists.

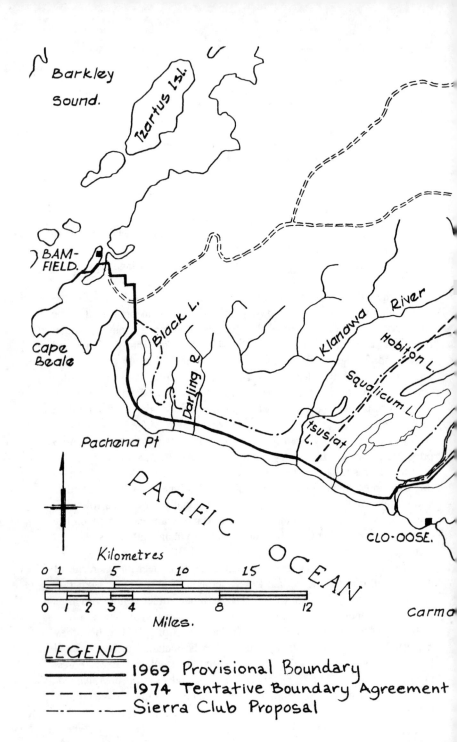

Barkley Sound.

Izartus Isl.

BAM-FIELD.

Cape Beale

Black L.

Darling R.

Klanawa River

Hobiton L.

Squalicum L.

Tsusiat L.

Pachena Pt

CLO-OOSE.

PACIFIC OCEAN

Carma

Kilometres

0 1   5   10   15

0   1   2   3   4   8   12

Miles.

LEGEND

———— 1969 Provisional Boundary

— — — — 1974 Tentative Boundary Agreement

—..——..— Sierra Club Proposal

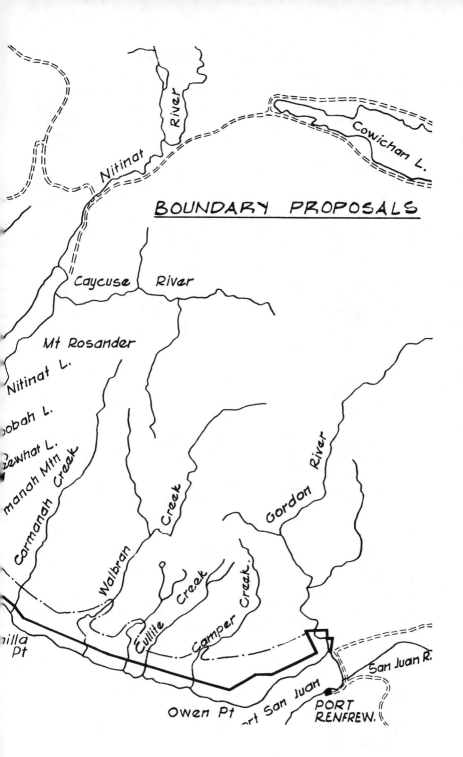

BOUNDARY PROPOSALS

River

Nitinat

Cowichan L.

Caycuse River

Mt Rosander

Nitinat L.

obah L.

ewhat L.

manah Mtn

Carmanah Creek

Creek

Gordon River

Walbran

Eullile Creek

Camper Creek

illa Pt

San Juan R.

Owen Pt

rt San Juan

PORT RENFREW.

Let us examine first why wider boundaries are needed for the West Coast Trail. Originally the only protected land was the narrow coastal strip, which would have allowed logging roads to be built within half a mile of the coast along almost the total length of the trail. A half mile buffer is far too slim to prevent trails being pushed through from the logging roads to such attractive spots as Carmanah Beach, Tsusiat and the Klanawa. The results are predictable: these areas would become heavily used and the trail would lose much of the natural and wild atmosphere which is its greatest charm. Rather than offering an opportunity for an extended communication with things natural, the journey would be cut up into a section of wild trail, an area of resident campers, and established campsites with all the accoutrements of motorized camping. The rare and unusual would be replaced by the commonplace.

To prevent this kind of intrusion the boundaries should have a minimum width of 1½ miles, a width of coastal scrub that should be enough to deter most unauthorized trail makers. By comparison, the Olympic Beach National Park in Washington State has an average width of over 2½ miles.

Such a width would also spare hikers much of the visual impact as well as the noise of the adjacent logging operations. In particular, the ocean face of Carmanah Mountain should not be logged; that face dominates many miles of the trail and the logging scars would spoil the natural beauty of the trail.

The argument for inclusion in the park of the Lower Klanawa, Black Lake, and other attractive spots is to add a variety of side trips from the main trail and to provide campsites situated off the main trail or beach.

The arguments for the preservation of the Nitinat Lakes are also related to rarity of experience. Hobiton, Tsusiat and Squalicum lakes offer safe canoe recreation not to be matched elsewhere on Vancouver Island. These extremely beautiful lakes are warm and at a low level. But the real impact of these lakes is in their forest. As you move up the Hobiton River to Hobiton Lake, the Hobiton-Tsusiat watershed opens up before you, a great sweep of forest rising from the lake up Hobiton Ridge, and you will be looking at virtually the last low-level accessible valley on Vancouver Island that is cloaked in its original virgin forest.

There are only two major watersheds of low-level west coast climax forest protected in British Columbia. The first is the Moyeha Valley in Strathcona Park, and its protection is in doubt because Strathcona has only Class B status and thus can be logged. The second is the ecological reserve on East Redonda Island, an area not open to the general public. Smaller portions at Cape Scott and Schoen Lake are also protected. All others are either presently being logged or are scheduled to be logged. The Moyeha is accessible only by boat or over a high mountain pass and is truly remote. The Nitinat forest is within three hours' travel of Victoria, yet many people are unaware of its existence.

To appreciate the impact of the Nitinat forest, it is important to understand its history and the changes which would be brought about if it were logged. In the coastal zone the forest moves through several transitions, known as stages of succession, before it reaches its climax state, when it can reproduce itself. After a major fire or after clearing, the pioneer species are usually shrubs, weeds and alder. These are followed by Douglas-fir, which cannot regenerate in shade. As fir ages and dies it is replaced by a cedar-hemlock forest which regenerates itself, the seedlings of these species being able to tolerate shade. Cedar-hemlock is thus the climax forest of the west coast. A Douglas-fir forest is considered temporary, where "temporary" is defined as lasting a thousand years or more. On the east coast of the island, fires historically prevented succession from going to the climax in most areas. (Logging now does the same thing in most parts of British Columbia outside of parks.) On the west coast and in some of the west central valleys of the island, rainfall made fire rare, and many forests have gone on for thousands of years.

Thus the low-level climax forest is a multi-age forest which may have taken up to 2,000 years to evolve. It is characterized by enormous trees, many of which are rotten; limited undergrowth, making travel easy, and a forest floor rich with small plants, mosses, lichens and many unusual fungi. Such a forest is described as "decadent" or "overmature" by industrial foresters, because older trees grow slowly and contain a high proportion of rot.

The replacement forest will have an entirely different character: for the first 20 years it will be virtually impenetrable as the young trees grow; for the next 20 years the stand will still be full of logging debris and the stems of young trees killed by competition with their neighbours; only in the last half of the cycle will the forest be attractive to the recreationist. During the first 40 years the richness of the forest floor will be gone, travel will be impeded by logging debris, and the great trees will be gone forever.

For a graphic example of this, drive to Cheewhat Lake, which is within the proposed park. A hundred-metre unlogged strip protects the lake, and beyond that it looks devastated. This is not abnormal — just usual west coast logging practice, and will take a decade or more to green up.

We advertise British Columbia as the tourists' paradise and boast of how the tourist industry will soon overtake the forest industry as a dollar earner, but we have not learned the obvious about the tourist: he does not travel to see what he can see at home — he travels to see the exceptional. The old climax forest of the Nitinat is exceptional; MacMillan Bloedel's uniform second growth is not. In the Nitinat and along the West Coast Trail the community appears not to recognize that the area has special values. The parallel might be if the French were to strip Notre Dame

TRAIL NEAR PACHENA

Cathedral of all its treasures and advertise for tourists to come and view the shell.

The Sierra Club of B. C. began a campaign in 1970 to make the public aware of the need to protect the Nitinat and West Coast Trail and to demonstrate that forest land has a high recreational value. The Club lobbied the Social Credit government vigorously and, through slides, film, speeches and books, took the issue to the public.

The Council of Forest Industries also lobbied strongly to prevent this precedent of land committed to commercial forestry being rezoned for recreation, and they had a good audience in the government. If the proposals of the National Park Branch and conservationists had been outrageous the CFI might have had a point, but the proposals were modest and the CFI arguments were weak. As an example, examine the effect of the loss to B. C. Forest Products of that portion of Tree Farm Licence 27 that lies in the Nitinat.

The Sierra Club asked that 14,000 acres be withdrawn from TFL 27, the Hobiton, Tsusiat and Squalicum drainages, of which 4,000 acres are lake and some further 2,000 acres around Tsusiat Lake carry only scrub and are poor growth sites.

If the loss of productive forest area is taken at 8,000 acres, then working on a sustained yield cycle of 80 years, the annual cut would have been only about 100 acres. Yet BCFP has a total annual cut in the province of over 10,000 acres. Thus its annual yield from the proposed park extension would amount to about only 1% of its annual intake of timber. It is fatuous to agree that such a small volume is essential to the operation of a major company which can obtain replacement timber by better utilization of timber from its other holdings.

BCFP stated that their major concern was to maintain employment at their Youbou mill, but some of their staff reported that only 15% of the timber supply for that mill came from the Nitinat and that the mill would have been closed in any event by 1982, for by then the company would have exhausted its other supplies of mature timber on Vancouver Island for which the mill was designed.

It is also interesting to note that BCFP and MacMillan Bloedel are two companies that have been criticized by the Forest Service for not adapting their mills fast enough to cope with the switch from old timber to second growth timber and, by this omission, for not utilizing the young second growth thinnings from their tree farm licences. If these were used in special mills, more employment would be created than would be lost by not logging the Nitinat. Only gradually are the big companies facing the inevitable conversion to logging smaller trees.

It can be stated confidently that the loss of the Nitinat created a minimum of difficulty for BCFP, yet the addition of the forests of the

Nitinat to the National Parks added something that could not be duplicated in Canada. A similar analysis for the proposed extractions from TFL 21 would show that they were not significant in the overall operations of MacMillan Bloedel.

There is a scientific gain by the inclusion of the Nitinat forest in the National Park. As yet we have preserved no complete drainage basins in their natural state in the coastal forests. We have accepted the word of the foresters that they can maintain a sustained harvest from our forests. Yet we know that each cutting cycle is accompanied by erosion of soil and nutrients. To check on the foresters' claims, some productive watersheds should be retained in an untouched state to be used as yardsticks against which the changes caused by forestry can be assessed. If science and recreation can be combined in this way, we will be fortunate. A proposal has already been made to include parts of the Nitinat forest in an ecological reserve to provide a benchmark for forest management.

The arguments of conservationists regarding park boundaries were resisted until a few days before the provincial election in 1972. At that time the Minister of Forests announced that the inclusion of the Hobiton-Tsusiat valley in the National Park was accepted in principle. After 1972 the elected government (the New Democratic Party) indicated that they would maintain their position in support of the inclusion of the Hobiton-Tsusiat valley in the National Park; thus the future of the magnificent forests of that valley seemed assured and the important precedent was set of land commmitted to forestry being rezoned for recreation. In 1974 the tentative boundaries were settled and were agreed to by the various government and industry parties; they form the basis for the negotiations which are still occurring. After 1975 the Social Credit government reconfirmed the provincial commitment.

Since then the meaning of the word "overcommitment" has become very clear. All parties concerned, including successive provincial governments, the federal government, and the two main logging companies have accepted the principle of wider boundaries for the trail and preservation of the Hobiton-Tsusiat watershed, as indeed they did years ago. The two main obstacles have been inflation and a lack of readily available lands with which to compensate the companies for loss of their cutting rights. Inflation was partially dealt with by the end of 1975 by way of a new cost-sharing agreement between the two levels of government. The subject of alternative lands is a much more difficult one. The best solution would be simply to admit that we have reached and perhaps exceeded the productivity limits of our forests, and begin to practice better utilization and conservation techniques. Unfortunately, a consumer-oriented society does not often think in those terms, nor does a major industry such as the forest products industry.

Negotiations between government and industry and between governments are still going on, with substitute lands having been found for the companies on Vancouver Island not involving removal of virgin forest from a park.

Some land has been removed from Phase I to give a logging corridor between Kennedy Lake and Long Beach, and the Kennedy Lake portion is now called Phase IV. In addition, there has been extensive logging in Strathcona Park, and a study has been occurring for several years now regarding revision to its boundaries. The result may be an increase in the amount of alpine and subalpine area but a decrease in the area of low level virgin forest. The pressures of logging on all the wilderness parks including those in Class A (fully protected) are tremendous and getting stronger. Even the Forest Service is now stating openly what conservation groups have been saying for several years: that the old growth forest is being cut at a faster rate than the new growth forest, under present management methods, can sustain. The necessity of adapting to lower rates of cut will occur at different times throughout B. C., but it is near. Cutting in the parks would provide miniscule help on a provincial scale, but would be significant to certain specific mills. At best it could only postpone the inevitable, and we would have lost a heritage which cannot be replaced in a lifetime. The long-term solution is intensive forestry and more efficient utilization of the product.

Once compensation for the companies is settled, the province will assemble the lands (including some private inholdings) and turn them over to the federal government. This may not occur for several years. The provincial government is currently demanding almost $100 million for the lands, while federal negotiators put the value at half that.

The 1974 boundary agreement has both positive and negative features. From Pachena Point to Tsocowis Creek the trail zone is almost a mile wide. There is good protection around the Hobiton-Tsusiat watershed, though Hitchie Lake will be almost accessible by road. The Clo-oose area is fairly well protected, except that logging will come close to Cheewhat Lake. From Logan Point to the Gordon River the zone is close to a mile in width. These widths, though not ideal, could be described as "satisfactory."

Other sections are less than satisfactory. Logging will come to within much less than a mile along some parts, and to within a quarter mile or less of the coast near Flat Rocks, and at a couple of places between Carmanah and the Walbran. Black Lake will probably be excluded from the park and the face of Carmanah Mountain will have logging visible for miles along the trail. There is no protection of the Klanawa, Carmanah or Walbran rivers; at the Klanawa especially the beach will be easily accessible by canoe. We hope that the final agreement will fix some of these weaknesses, and that the logging companies will restrict motorized access on those spur roads which come closest to the trail.

This book has been published to help you enjoy the West Coast Trail area, and to help you appreciate that a wilderness is a priceless and endangered resource.

We hope that you will make your views known to the politicians who are responsible for future decisions on our wilderness areas. The main ones are:

National park lands:
   Minister of the Environment,
   National Parks Branch,
   Parliament Buildings,
   Ottawa, Ontario.

Provincial lands outside parks:
   Minister of Forests and Lands,
   Parliament Buildings, Victoria, B.C.

Provincial lands within parks:
   Minister of Environment and Parks,
   Parliament Buildings, Victoria, B.C.

For more information on wilderness issues in Western Canada, or to give comments or suggestions about this book, write to the Sierra Club of Western Canada, Box 202, Victoria, B.C., 386-5255. The following Victoria numbers can also be phoned for information: 383-6790 or 595-0655.